Beyond the Statement

Also by Eden Gillott

A Lawyer's Guide to Crisis PR (with Roger Gillott)

A Board Member's Guide to Crisis PR (with Roger Gillott)

A Business Owner's Guide to Crisis PR (with Roger Gillott)

Beyond the Statement

Strategic Leadership When Everything's at Stake

Eden Gillott

Beyond the Statement

First Edition 2025
ISBN-13: 978-0-9912480-9-4
www.gillottcommunications.com

DEDICATION

To Roger

CONTENTS

INTRODUCTION

Here's an uncomfortable truth: Most companies devote more effort to crisis response than to crisis prevention. It's human nature. We react more strongly to immediate threats than to potential ones. In Crisis PR, that's a recipe for disaster.

But not you.

If you're reading this, it means you value protecting the company's reputation.

Throughout this book, I primarily use "Crisis PR" when focusing on communication tactics, "Crisis Management" when addressing the integrated organizational response, and "Reputation Management" when discussing the broader, ongoing process of shaping how stakeholders perceive your company. However, the most crucial principle transcends terminology: whatever you call this work, it requires integrating strategic thinking, operational excellence, and authentic communication to protect your company's most valuable intangible asset: its reputation.

HOW TO USE THIS BOOK

Crises don't operate on a convenient schedule, nor should your approach to this book. I've designed *Beyond the Statement* to serve multiple purposes: from preparation before crises hit to rapid guidance when you're facing reputation challenges. Here's how to get the most from these pages, depending on your current situation:

If You're Not Currently Facing a Crisis

Congratulations! This is precisely when you should be preparing. Here's your roadmap:

For the Strategic Builder: Read the book from start to finish before exploring specific scenarios. The chapters build logically on each other, creating a framework for crisis prevention and response.

For the Framework Seeker: Focus on the assessment tools, matrices, and decision frameworks scattered throughout each chapter. These practical tools form the backbone of effective crisis management. Identify the frameworks that most closely apply to your organization and begin implementing them immediately.

For the Culture Architect: Pay special attention to Chapters 6 and 9, which focus on building crisis-resistant cultures. The Five Pillars of Crisis-Resistant Culture and the executive mindset preparation sections provide the foundation for organizations to prevent crises rather than just manage them.

For the Case Study Learner: Some chapters end with detailed client case studies that demonstrate the real-world application of the principles discussed. These stories reveal how organizations succeeded (or failed) in applying these concepts across different industries and situations. Study these examples to internalize the patterns of effective crisis management. Micro client case studies are also sprinkled throughout for quick hits of context and color. Disclaimer: While I've changed identifying details to protect client confidentiality, these case studies are drawn from real crises I've managed throughout my career. "Masterclass Moments" are public examples that are also woven into the chapters.

If You're in the Middle of a Crisis Right Now

First, take a deep breath. Then, pick up the phone and call your Crisis Management strategist. Don't waste valuable time researching and trying to implement things for the first time on your own.

If you've already called them and you want to brush up before the initial strategy session, then:

For Immediate Guidance: Start with the Strategic Response Framework in Chapter 1 to assess your situation, then jump to the chapter most relevant to your current stage:

- **Just discovered the issue?** → Chapter 2: The Anatomy of a Crisis
- **Deciding when/how to respond?** → Chapter 3: The Power of the Pause
- **Crafting your message?** → Chapter 4: Strategic Narrative Architecture
- **Leading through chaos?** → Chapter 6: Leadership Under Fire

- **Managing stakeholder reactions?** → Chapter 7: Navigating Public Perception

For Quick Reference: The executive summaries at the start of each chapter provide crucial principles in condensed form for when you need guidance fast. The checklists and frameworks throughout the book offer step-by-step approaches when you don't have time to read entire chapters.

A NOTE ON CASE STUDIES

Each case study follows the whole arc of a crisis, from initial trigger through resolution and lessons learned, and is structured to highlight the crucial elements:

- **Crisis Trigger**: What sparked the situation
- **Initial Response**: The first critical hours
- **Strategic Approach**: Key decisions and their rationale
- **Implementation Challenges**: What made execution difficult
- **Resolution Path**: How the situation was ultimately resolved
- **Outcome Analysis**: Measuring success and impact
- **Lessons Learned**: Key takeaways applicable to other situations

As you read these case studies, look for the patterns that emerge across different scenarios. These reveal the fundamental truths of effective crisis management that transcend industry, situation, and context.

A NOTE ON IMPLEMENTATION

Crisis management isn't just about knowing what to do; it's about building the muscle memory to execute effectively under pressure. Don't just read this book; use it as a guide for implementing specific practices in your organization:

- **Select your priority frameworks** from across the chapters based on your organization's particular needs.
- **Develop implementation plans** to integrate these capabilities into your operations.
- **Practice regularly** through simulations and tabletop exercises to enhance your skills.
- **Revisit key chapters** as your organization evolves or faces new challenges.

Remember, the time to prepare is *now,* before the crisis arrives. But even if you're currently in the middle of reputation challenges, the principles and frameworks in these pages can help you navigate to safer shores.

Let's begin.

CHAPTER 1
UNMASKING THE CRISIS PR
MYTHS

EXECUTIVE SUMMARY

The most prominent myths in Crisis PR lead to the most common failures.

This chapter dismantles three dangerous myths that plague crisis management:

- A perfect statement alone can fix any situation
- Faster is always better when responding
- The crisis is over when the headlines stop

Through real-world examples, you'll learn how strategic assessment, stakeholder analysis, and long-term reputation management are the true foundations of effective crisis management. This chapter presents a Strategic Response Framework that helps you assess the situation, map key stakeholders, and establish suitable timelines for response.

It was a Sunday evening. I'd been on a kick to learn how to become a better cook. I was raised in a household that relied heavily on SPAM®, Kraft Mac & Cheese, TV dinners, fast food, and local restaurants. And on the rare occasion we hosted a holiday, it was catered by Honey Baked Ham or Giuliano's Delicatessen and put onto platters as if we'd made it ourselves, à la Robin Williams in *Mrs. Doubtfire*. I then spent most of my professional career trying to live by Keith Ferrazzi's *Never Eat Alone* approach to building your network and, as a result, ended up with a fridge that looked like I'd just moved in the day before.

So, I'm elbows-deep trying to recreate something from Mark Bittman's *How to Cook Everything* cookbook and cursing the fact that I didn't appreciate the idea of taking Home Ec (a.k.a. Home Economics) in high school when I had the chance, when my phone starts blowing up with back-to-back frantic messages. First, an email, followed by a text, and a call, all within five minutes.

"Eden, everything is falling apart. We need to put out a statement. RIGHT. NOW."

I've received this kind of panicked call hundreds, if not thousands, of times throughout my career. The details change, but the core response is always the same: "Let's just put out a statement." It's the corporate equivalent of putting a Band-Aid on a massive gash in a ship's hull.

#1 THE MYTH OF "I JUST NEED A STATEMENT"

Behind almost every crisis call I receive lies the same hope: that there's a quick fix. Specifically, that there's a perfect statement that will make everything go away.

I get it.

You want immediate action when your reputation is on the line (whether or not the media is breathing down your neck). But here's what folks outside my industry don't know: the statement everyone sees is just the tip of the iceberg.

As Boromir so aptly put it in *The Lord of the Rings*, "One does not simply walk into Mordor." And in crisis management? One does not simply statement their way out of a reputational threat.

The strategic heavy lifting that determines success or failure happens <u>long</u> before anyone types a single word. That's the *real* work.

Like the first and second rules in *Fight Club*[1], the first and second rules of Damage Control are: You do not do more damage. (Repeat: You DO NOT do more damage.) However, that's precisely what happens when organizations rush to issue a statement without establishing a proper strategic foundation. They're essentially trying to build a house, starting with the front door.

THE STRATEGIC REALITY

Crisis PR is like an iceberg: the statement everyone sees is just the 10% that's above water. The other 90% is:

- Strategic assessment
- Stakeholder analysis
- Risk evaluation
- Message architecture
- Implementation planning

- Long-term reputation management

Let me share a story that never made headlines. That's precisely why it's successful. A non-profit discovered financial irregularities just before its biggest fundraising event of the year. Their first instinct? You guessed it: put out a statement explaining the situation.

Instead, we:

- Conducted a swift internal audit
- Developed a comprehensive action plan
- Created targeted communications for different stakeholders
- Implemented new financial controls
- Prepared crisis-prevention protocols

The result? The situation was handled so smoothly that it never became public. The fundraiser was a success, and the organization emerged stronger and more profitable than before.

2 THE MYTH OF FASTER IS BETTER

A new mom began breastfeeding in a client's high-end retail store. Nothing out of the ordinary or inappropriate.

The owner politely let the mom know she was on candid camera (actually, 200 high-def surveillance ones) and that if she'd prefer privacy, lounges were available. The mom said she was fine and shopped happily for the next hour.

But as soon as she left, the mom called her lawyer, claiming she was illegally discouraged and bullied from breastfeeding in the store.

Within hours, the mommy-sphere was in an uproar. The new mom had taken her version of the story to the internet and mobilized a large, passionate audience. Yelp. Mommy blogs. Facebook groups. Friends. Friends-of-friends. The media. There was even a talk of a well-publicized "nurse-in."

Instead of rushing out a defensive statement, we:

- Quickly questioned everyone involved. Time is tricky because it muddles memories. Events get reinterpreted, and facts get forgotten.
- Crafted strategic responses that set the story straight.
- Took the battle directly to where it started, online, by posting some publicly and others as private messages.
- Guided media to our carefully constructed narrative. (Note: Depending on the situation, we sometimes refer the media to a statement instead of trying to coordinate an interview and do any necessary media training beforehand.)

The result? No news items ran because we made it a non-story. The accuser admitted it was a misunderstanding and removed her negative posts. Some critics even became customers. That's the power of strategy over speed.

STRATEGIC RESPONSE FRAMEWORK

Before you even *think* about crafting a statement, you need to understand what you're really dealing with. Here's the Strategic Response Framework I've refined over two decades of managing crises:

Impact Assessment

- How serious is the situation?
- Who's affected?
- What's at stake?

Stakeholder Mapping

- Who needs to hear from us?
- What do they need to know?
- How will they likely react?

Response Timeline

- What must happen in the next hour?
- The next day?
- The following week?

This initial framework provides the foundation for our more detailed approach to communicating with your stakeholders in Chapter 2, where we'll examine how to identify and prioritize different audience segments during each phase. We'll also revisit the Response Timeline element when we explore the power of strategic silence in Chapter 3, demonstrating how timing considerations shape effective crisis management. We'll also meet the product manufacturer who employs this initial framework in Chapter 4, when facing potentially contaminated products and needing time to conduct proper testing before determining their course of action.

DON'T MISTAKE INACTION FOR INACTIVITY

Some people thrive on action, whether doing it or watching it. If you're not in motion, you're deemed to be doing nothing.

Long ago, when Roger, founder of Gillott Communications, was sitting in for the hyperactive city editor at The Associated Press, the news editor scolded him for not appearing busy. After being assured that all relevant stories had been assigned and reporters were working on them, the news editor walked away, not wholly convinced and still grumbling suspiciously.

Clients sometimes view Crisis Management in the same light.

"This is the worst thing that's ever happened."

> *"Why are you spending time talking to us instead of fixing the problem?"*

"Why aren't you doing something this instant?"

> *"Why can't you make it better right now?"*

Notice a trend? A desire for an instant cure. A sense that if you're not breaking a sweat, you mustn't be doing your job.

Let's compare the client's statements with reality.

This may be the worst thing that's ever happened to the client. Something the company or non-profit never had to face before. That's unnerving. That's also why they brought in an outside Crisis Management strategist familiar with such matters.

Why do we ask so many initial questions about the situation and back story? Because we must know where all the skeletons are buried to do our job effectively. To be armed with half-truths and lies can destroy your reputation.

Why aren't you making it better this very instant? If you're good at your job, you exude calm. You need to gather information before developing an initial strategy. *Only then* can you refine tactics to steer the situation in the direction that's achievable and most beneficial to the client.

Jumping into action without thinking first about what you're looking to achieve and the possible (unintended) consequences is a recipe for disaster. This includes issuing statements without facts or ensuring that what you say or do is aligned with your overall goal.

3 THE MYTH THAT THE CRISIS IS OVER WHEN THE HEADLINES & SOCIAL MEDIA FLURRY STOP

If you think the crisis is over when the (social) media moves on, I'm sorry to be the bearer of bad news. The headlines are just the beginning. The real work of rebuilding trust and strengthening your organization has only just begun.

I once had a client celebrate when their crisis stopped trending on Twitter and decided to return to business as usual, despite having a plan for some course corrections that would be better for the long term. Two weeks later, they felt blindsided by the second wave: customer boycotts, employee resignations, and shareholder concerns. They learned the hard way that managing a crisis is a marathon, not a sprint. With my urging, they quickly resumed our original plan.

Here's what most people don't understand about Crisis PR: The crisis isn't over when the headlines stop. That's often just the beginning. Your real work is rebuilding trust, strengthening relationships, implementing changes, and preventing future issues.

DON'T FORSAKE LONG-TERM SUCCESS FOR SHORT-TERM GAINS

Mutual fund guru John Bogle shared Warren Buffett's philosophy: chasing short-term gain is a fool's errand. Capturing intrinsic value is the real prize.

In our world, the calculus differs only slightly. You can't ignore the crisis that's staring you in the face. That would be foolhardy. You must deal with it in the moment.

But you must never take your eyes off the horizon. Are the tone and the message right for the long term? How will the public perceive your organization next week, month, or year?

The rule is straightforward: Winning a fight is nice. Winning the war is better.

Some clients get it instinctively. Others must be guided.

Business executives are a good example. Those who quickly grasp the dynamics of guarding a reputation are the same who embrace the concepts that former Intel CEO Andy Grove identified in his book, *Only the Paranoid Survive*: Beating the competition with one product or for one season is temporary.

You must always be alert for "inflection points": forces beyond your control that will reshape your industry. If you recognize and anticipate them, you'll profit. If you don't, you'll stumble and lose.

The best executives and Crisis Management team have no tolerance for wasting time. They think fast, decide fast, and act fast.

In one case, a complex Reputation Management concept was being laid out for a CEO. Thirty seconds into what was to be a 3-minute presentation, he waved to halt. "I see where you're going. Do it. Anything else?"

Such abruptness is both chastening and reassuring. (It can be daunting to those unaccustomed to fast minds, but it means you have the client's confidence.)

However, a caveat lurks not far below the surface: Make no mistakes. If any slip-up occurs in executing your plan, that confidence will quickly evaporate.

We've explored three dangerous myths: that statements alone can fix crises, that faster is always better, and that the crisis ends when headlines stop. These myths can be seen in nearly every organizational failure we'll examine throughout this book. You'll revisit our luxury retailer in Chapter 3 because they initially began drafting a defensive statement before realizing the power of strategic assessment. Similarly, a company in Chapter 2 and a CEO in Chapter 4 both discovered that gathering facts and aligning their teams produced far better outcomes than rushing to respond to the situation. As we'll see repeatedly, strategic patience often outperforms reactive speed.

CONCLUSION

Effective Crisis PR goes far beyond crafting the perfect statement. It requires strategic thinking, stakeholder analysis, and a comprehensive approach that addresses both immediate needs and long-term reputation management.

Remember the three critical myths we've debunked:

- The "just need a statement" myth overlooks the strategic foundation necessary for success
- The "faster is better" myth prioritizes speed over accuracy and effectiveness
- The "crisis ends when headlines stop" myth ignores the vital work of rebuilding trust

These myths persist because they offer the comfort of simplicity in chaotic situations. As we've seen, Crisis PR isn't about having the perfect words. It's about having the right strategy. The statement everyone sees is just the visible tip of a much larger iceberg of preparation, assessment, and strategic thinking.

But how do you know what stage of a crisis you're in or what warning signs to watch for before situations escalate? In the next chapter, we'll dissect the anatomy of a crisis and understand its triggers, stages, and psychological impacts so you can recognize the signs *before* they escalate into full-blown reputational threats. Just as doctors need to understand human anatomy to treat patients effectively, crisis professionals need to understand crisis physiology to manage reputation threats.

CHAPTER 2
THE ANATOMY OF A CRISIS

EXECUTIVE SUMMARY

Crises follow predictable patterns (for the most part). Learn to spot the early warning signs, and you can stop problems before they explode into full-blown disasters.

By understanding these patterns, you can respond more strategically. This chapter maps these patterns through the Crisis Assessment Matrix. It identifies the distinct phases every crisis moves through: Detective Mode (Hours 1-24), The Critical Window (Hours 24-48), The Shockwave Period (48+ hours), The Monitoring & Adjustment Phase (Week 1+), The Aftershock(s) Phase (Week 2+), and The Recovery & Reform Stage (Months 2-6). By understanding the psychological and operational dimensions of each phase, you can anticipate challenges and implement the right strategies at the right moments.

You know that scene in *Jurassic Park* when the kids are stuck in the Jeep in the pouring rain. First, they hear this sound they don't quite recognize, so their attention starts to perk up. Next, they notice small ripples in the water glass and see the rearview mirror shaking before they start trying to guess what it might be. Then, once they notice the goat in the nearby enclosure is missing, they finally begin to grasp the severity of the situation.

Crisis management is the same vibe. There are always warning signs: tiny ripples that tell you something big is coming. Crisis management isn't just about putting out fires; it's about:

- Understanding patterns
- Anticipating reactions
- Building resilience
- Creating systems
- Learning constantly

THE EARLY WARNING SIGNS SYSTEM

Crisis triggers come in two flavors:

External (The Meteor)

- Sudden market changes
- Natural disasters
- Competitor actions
- Regulatory changes
- Social media explosions

Internal (The Time Bomb)

- Poor management decisions
- Weak protocols
- Information leaks
- Company culture issues

- Operational shortcuts

Organizations that invest in identifying early warning signals can often address potential crises while they are still in the "ripples in the water" stage rather than waiting until they face the full T-Rex of a major reputation threat. We'll explore how to build these early warning capabilities into your organizational culture when we discuss crisis-resistant cultures in Chapter 9.

THE CRISIS ASSESSMENT MATRIX

Rate each factor on a scale of 1-5 (think spice level at your favorite Thai or Indian restaurant). After completing the assessment, calculate your total score and refer to the Crisis Threat Level guide to determine the severity of your situation and the appropriate response level. This will feel very familiar for all my Cosmopolitan magazine girlies, *except* this is packed with useful advice instead of less-than-subtle ways of making you insecure about yourself to sell you more beauty products.

Immediacy *How fast is this moving? The more time-sensitive, the higher the number.*

Slow Simmer: Developing over weeks or months with no immediate pressure *(1 point)*

Gentle Boil: Building gradually with time to plan a thoughtful response *(2 points)*

Rolling Boil: Accelerating with clear momentum but still manageable *(3 points)*

21

Rapid Boil: Moving quickly with limited time for comprehensive assessment *(4 points)*

Flash Point: Exploding in real-time with immediate response required *(5 points)*

Questions to consider:

- How quickly is information spreading?
- Are stakeholders demanding immediate responses?
- Is there a hard deadline or event that will force the issue?
- Is traditional or social media already covering this?
- Are competitors or opponents driving the timeline?

Scope *Who's affected? The more people who are impacted and the higher their importance to the company, the higher the number.*

Isolated: Affects a small, non-critical stakeholder group *(1 point)*

Limited: Impacts a defined segment of stakeholders but not core groups *(2 points)*

Significant: Touches important stakeholder groups but not comprehensively *(3 points)*

Extensive: Affects multiple critical stakeholder groups simultaneously *(4 points)*

Universal: Impacts virtually all key stakeholders across the organization *(5 points)*

Questions to consider:

- Which stakeholder groups are directly affected?
- How important are these groups to your organization's success?
- Are there potential ripple effects on other stakeholder groups?
- Does this cross departmental or divisional boundaries?
- Could this expand to affect stakeholders who are currently not impacted?

Severity *How bad is it? The more severe, the higher the number.*

Mild Discomfort: Annoying but causing minimal actual harm *(1 point)*

Moderate Pain: Creating real problems but not existential threats *(2 points)*

Serious Concern: Causing significant damage requiring major attention *(3 points)*

Critical Condition: Threatening fundamental aspects of the organization *(4 points)*

Catastrophic: Posing existential threats to organizational survival *(5 points)*

Questions to consider:

- What's the potential financial impact?

- Could this affect organizational leadership stability?
- Is the organization's fundamental mission or license to operate at risk?
- What's the potential long-term reputation damage?
- Could this create regulatory, legal, or criminal exposure?

Visibility *Who knows? The more people who know and the higher their importance to the company, the higher the number.*

Internal Only: Known only within a limited organizational circle *(1 point)*

Partial Exposure: Visible to some external stakeholders but not widely known *(2 points)*

Public Awareness: Known publicly but not yet receiving significant attention *(3 points)*

High Profile: Receiving substantial public and media attention *(4 points)*

Spotlight: Dominating news cycles and public conversation *(5 points)*

Questions to consider:

- Are influential stakeholders aware of and discussing it?
- What's the search visibility when looking for your organization?

- Has this appeared in traditional or social media yet?
- Are employees discussing this with people outside the organization?
- Is this likely to attract investigative journalism or regulatory attention?

Control *What can we influence? The less you can control, the higher the number.*

High Control: Organization has a significant ability to direct outcomes *(1 point)*

Moderate Control: Can influence main elements but not all aspects *(2 points)*

Limited Control: Can affect some crucial factors but not the core issue *(3 points)*

Minimal Control: Can only influence peripheral elements of the situation *(4 points)*

No Control: Completely at the mercy of external forces and decisions *(5 points)*

Questions to consider:

- Do you own the original source of the problem?
- Can you directly address the root causes?
- How much do external actors control the narrative?
- Are legal, regulatory, or other constraints limiting your options?
- Do you have relationships with key decision-makers in this situation?

Scoring Your Crisis

5-10: Low-Level Concern

Approach: Measured and Methodical

You have time to develop a comprehensive approach. Focus on thorough assessment and preventative measures to keep the situation from escalating. Document your process and prepare contingency plans in case the situation intensifies.

11-15: Emerging Issue

Approach: Proactive Management

The situation requires attention, but not emergency measures. Assign a dedicated team to monitor developments and prepare response options. Begin stakeholder mapping and develop preliminary messaging frameworks while continuing assessment.

16-20: Active Crisis

Approach: Focused Response

You're facing a legitimate crisis requiring dedicated resources and leadership attention. Activate your crisis team, establish regular assessment cycles, and implement your crisis communications plan. Develop both immediate response and mid-term recovery strategies.

21-24: Critical Situation

Approach: Intensive Intervention

This high-severity crisis demands immediate, focused attention from senior leadership. Consider suspending normal operations in affected areas and establishing a dedicated crisis command center to manage the situation effectively. Implement 24-hour monitoring and response capabilities, accompanied by regular leadership briefings.

25+: Organizational Emergency

Approach: All-Hands Response

You're facing a potential existential threat that requires extraordinary measures. Activate your highest-level crisis protocols with direct involvement from the CEO. Consider bringing in external expertise immediately and establishing round-the-clock operations to ensure optimal performance. Your focus must be on immediate stabilization and long-term survival.

Dimension Analysis

Beyond your total score, pay special attention to individual dimensions scoring 4 or 5, as these represent critical vulnerabilities requiring targeted strategies:

High Immediacy (4-5): Prioritize rapid response protocols and real-time monitoring systems. Consider pre-approved messaging templates (with tailoring, obvi.) and a designated spokesperson (with a backup, also obvi.) who can respond without waiting until the last minute for lengthy approval processes.

High Scope (4-5): Implement comprehensive stakeholder mapping and develop segmented communication plans tailored to the specific concerns and needs of each affected group.

High Severity (4-5): Ensure senior leadership involvement and consider assembling specialized expertise (legal, regulatory, technical) specific to the threat. Develop scenario planning for worst-case outcomes.

High Visibility (4-5): Establish centralized message control, media monitoring, and coordinated spokesperson protocols. Consider proactive outreach to key influencers who can help shape the narrative.

High Control Challenges (4-5): Focus on relationship building with external decision-makers and developing influence strategies rather than direct control approaches. Prepare for multiple scenarios based on possible external actions.

Crisis Profile Patterns

The specific pattern across dimensions often reveals more than the total score. Watch for these common profiles:

The Sleeper Crisis: *Low Immediacy (1-2), Low Visibility (1-2), High Severity (4-5)* These situations appear manageable but have catastrophic potential if not addressed. Strategy: Use the available time to thoroughly address root causes before visibility increases.

The Media Firestorm: *High Immediacy (5), High Visibility (5), Low Severity (1-2)* These look worse than they are due to intense but typically short-lived media attention. Strategy: Weather the initial storm with calm leadership while maintaining perspective on the limited actual impact.

The Systemic Threat: *High Scope (4-5), High Severity (4-5), Low Control (4-5)* These fundamental challenges to your operations require transformative approaches. Strategy: Focus on organizational adaptation rather than just crisis communications.

The Emerging Scandal: *Low Immediacy (1-2), Low Visibility (1-2), Low Control (4-5)* These situations will likely become public eventually, with timing outside your control. Strategy: Use available time to develop comprehensive response plans and strengthen resilience.

Re-assess your crisis dimensions regularly as situations evolve, particularly watching for changes in Immediacy and Visibility that may signal a need to escalate your response approach.

BEHIND THE SCENES: THE FIRST HOURS OF A CRISIS

You receive a call. Something's gone horribly wrong, and everyone is demanding answers. Tiny beads of sweat form on your face. You feel a rush of heat all over your body.

Time stands still.

What do you need to do?

Let me take you behind the curtain of those crucial first hours of a crisis. While everyone else is screaming, "Put out a statement!" here's what should *actually* be happening:

Ideally, you've established a crisis team in advance, making the initial minutes smoother. Regrettably, clients too often haven't thought even this far ahead, so the situation is chaotic. (You, on the other hand, are very proactive and will be prepared. I mean, you're reading this book already, right?)

For those who do have a crisis team, it should include:

- **CEO, COO, CFO** They're the ones ultimately responsible for running the ship.
- **In-house or outside legal counsel** Attorneys are critical. Their role is to ensure that whatever you say or do is protected and that you don't make the situation worse from a legal perspective.
- **In-house communications director and outside crisis communications consultant** They work hand-in-hand. If your in-house communications person feels like they're in over their head, the outside consultant can take the lead and strengthen the team.
- **Human Resources** This is especially important when the situation involves a personnel issue. (Hint: It almost ALWAYS involves a personnel issue.)

- **Head of IT or outside IT security consultant** If it's a cybersecurity issue, your head of IT (as talented as they are) may not be as familiar with such matters.
- **Insurance agent** Your insurance may cover crisis expenses. Your agent can ensure you don't do something that voids your coverage. This can save money and headaches.

You must gather, vet, and synthesize information. Separate facts from rumors and speculation. This is an ongoing process.

Your analysis will guide you in grappling with key questions:

- What happened?
- What didn't happen (but should've)?
- Who knew what and when? What's being said publicly? What are the perceptions?
- What's likely to happen next?
- What's your goal? (Not how to achieve it; that comes later.)
- What are your options? What are the likely implications of each option?

This provides the foundation. Only *then* can you create your initial strategy. As new information floods in, that strategy may need to be adjusted. You must always be ready to pivot quickly. But if you did your initial analysis correctly, you won't need to reverse course or backpedal. And whatever the situation, it's <u>never</u> okay to lie.

Now that you know the facts and what you want to achieve, you can figure out how to get there. (See, I promised we'd get to it.)

- Who's your audience?
- What's your message?
- What's the best way to deliver it?
- Who should deliver it?

Your plan must be straightforward. Everyone needs to understand their responsibilities. You can't anticipate everything, but your team must be ready to act on whatever and whenever it occurs. No time for duplicating efforts, dropping the ball, or glaring holes in coverage.

Most of all, you must be calm. Customers, the public, and the media can sense nervousness. That creates an undesirable perception of uncertainty and weakness, which undermines trust.

Always remember: The first things you say and do set the tone for everything that follows, especially in a crisis.

DETECTIVE MODE: HOURS 1-24

Sometimes, Detective Mode is fast (maybe an hour or two) because the situation is clear-cut and the client's more proactive-minded and therefore prepared. But sometimes, Detective Mode is condensed because they hit a wall when trying to answer "What's missing?" and need to bring in an outside investigator. Other times, it takes closer to a full day because they need to gain access to the right people or systems.

Key Questions:

- What happened? (Facts)
- Who knew what and when? (Timeline)
- What's public? (Exposure)
- What's coming? (Threats)
- What's missing? (Gaps)

Emotional Temperature Check

While you're gathering facts, you need to simultaneously track emotional responses. Think of it like taking vital signs during triage.

Stakeholder Emotion Mapping:

- Employees: Are they afraid? Angry? Confused?
- Customers: Do they feel betrayed? Concerned? Indifferent?
- Partners: Are they nervous? Supportive? Distancing?
- Public: Is there outrage? Curiosity? Sympathy?

For example, during a data breach at a healthcare company, we noticed that employees were more concerned about losing their jobs than about the breach itself. This completely changed our internal communication strategy.

Emotion Tracking Tools:

- Internal chat monitoring, including water cooler convos
- Employee hotline feedback

- Social media sentiment analysis
- Customer service call themes
- Media tone assessment

This stakeholder emotion mapping builds upon the Strategic Response Framework introduced in Chapter 1 and provides essential context for the Three Levels of Empathy approach we'll explore in Chapter 7. Understanding emotional dynamics at each crisis stage creates the foundation for effective leadership during high-pressure situations, which we'll examine in detail in Chapter 6.

THE CRITICAL WINDOW: HOURS 24-48

The Critical Window begins immediately after Detective Mode ends, which, in many cases, with our proactive clients, is only a few hours after they realize something has gone wrong or has the potential to go sideways.

This is where amateurs and pros part ways. You need to:

- Verify all information
- Map stakeholder impacts (usually done mentally)
- Develop a response strategy (often done mentally)
- Prepare communications (this is where the drafting begins)
- Begin implementation

Stakeholder Psychology Deep Dive

Different stakeholders process information differently during crises. This is where understanding psychological responses becomes crucial.

Primary Stakeholders:

- Employees seek security
- Customers want reassurance
- Investors need confidence
- Partners require clarity

Secondary Stakeholders:

- Media wants a narrative
- Public seeks justice
- Regulators demand compliance
- Activists pursue change

Let me tell you about a manufacturing company that got this exactly right. During a significant product recall, they recognized that their business customers needed data and logistics while end-users needed empathy and support. They created two distinct communication streams, each addressing the psychological needs of their audience.

THE SHOCKWAVE PERIOD: 48+ HOURS

The Shockwave Period begins immediately after implementation is rolled out and the initial news is released (whether that's internally, externally, or both).

During this period, you'll experience things like:

- New stakeholders coming forward (This is most common when there have been allegations of sexual misconduct, and the person in question is still in denial. If you've done a thorough enough investigation, this won't be the case.)
- Employee morale changes surface
- Customer behavior changes manifest
- Supply chain/partner impacts appear
- Media coverage evolves
- Market responds

Perception Management System

This is where you actively shape how your crisis response is received and interpreted. Think of it as conducting an orchestra where different sections need different directions at various times.

The Three Levels of Perception:

- **Immediate Perception**

  - What are people saying?
  - How are they reacting?
  - Where are they expressing it?

- **Developing Narrative**

  - Which stories are emerging?
  - Who's shaping them?
  - How are they spreading?

- **Long-term Impact**

  - What's likely to stick?
  - Which changes are needed?
  - How to reshape the story?

I worked with a tech company facing privacy concerns. Their initial instinct was to focus on technical fixes. However, our perception tracking showed that people were less concerned about the technical details and more worried about feeling violated. We counseled the client to focus on rebuilding trust rather than explaining security protocols.

THE MONITORING & ADJUSTMENT PHASE: Week 1+

While you constantly monitor and make adjustments when needed during the earlier phases, during this phase, you'll primarily track the effectiveness of your initial strategy (and any adjustments you've made thus far).

This typically includes gauging stakeholder sentiment: direct feedback, watching as the media coverage trends change, and monitoring social media conversations. You'll also be looking at impacts on business metrics.

Response Impact Assessment

Track how your response is affecting stakeholder psychology:

Emotional Evolution Indicators:

- Shift from anger to understanding
- Movement from fear to confidence
- Transition from outrage to acceptance

Perception Shift Markers:

- Media tone changes
- Comment section themes
- Employee feedback patterns
- Customer interaction quality

THE AFTERSHOCK(S) PHASE: Week 2+

Two major parts of this phase are addressing emerging concerns and handling secondary issues.

Emerging concerns involve handling new worries that bubble up as the initial crisis unfolds. For example:

- Customers raise questions about other products after one product has issues
- Investors spot potential problems in other areas of the business
- Stakeholders bring up historical incidents that seem similar (the media loves a trend, so this often comes out when they've done their digging)
- Former employees come forward with related stories (again, the media will jump all over this)

Psychological Aftershocks

Just like earthquakes have aftershocks, crises have psychological reverberations:

Common Patterns:

- Trust testing (stakeholders watching for consistency)
- Reality checks (people comparing words to actions)
- Memory triggers (similar events causing anxiety)
- Progressive processing (delayed emotional responses)

Secondary issues are triggered by or exposed because of the initial crisis. These are usually dealt with in earlier phases, such as Detective Mode or Critical Window, but sometimes, they're deemed backburner issues due to a company's constraints. These include things like:

- A product recall reveals flaws in your quality control system
- A cyber breach exposes outdated IT infrastructure
- A leadership scandal uncovers broader cultural problems
- A facility accident highlights systemic safety violations
- A financial irregularity reveals weak internal controls

Three weeks after their crisis, the CEO of a hospital noticed a spike in employee anxiety. Not because anything new had happened, but because people were finally processing the emotional impact of the original event.

THE RECOVERY & REFORM STAGE: Months 2-6

This is where you need to make good on your promises. Like a game of Chutes and Ladders, falter here, and you'll end up tumbling back down to where you started.

- Implement systemic changes
- Update policies and procedures
- Conduct staff training
- Rebuild stakeholder trust
- Restore brand reputation
- Strengthen vulnerable areas
- Document lessons learned
- Create prevention protocols

Psychological Recovery Plan

True recovery is about fixing systems and healing the psychological wounds.

Recovery Indicators:

- Trust rebuilding milestones
- Relationship repair markers
- Confidence restoration signs
- Loyalty return signals

Reform Success Metrics:

- Stakeholder feedback quality

- Engagement level changes
- Relationship strength indicators
- Trust measurement scores

It's important to understand that emotional recovery often lags behind operational recovery. One retail chain I worked with had its systems fixed in two months, but it took six months of consistent action before customer trust returned to pre-crisis levels.

Remember: You're not just managing a crisis. You're managing human psychology at scale. Be patient.

THE STAKEHOLDER LEVELS

Picture your crisis response like the Earth's strata:

- Inner Core (Employees, Board)
- Outer Core (Customers, Partners)
- Mantle (Media, Public)
- Crust (Industry, Regulators)

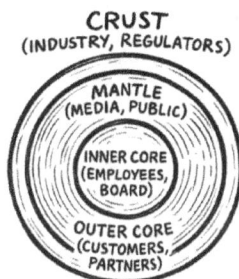

CRUST
(INDUSTRY, REGULATORS)

MANTLE
(MEDIA, PUBLIC)

INNER CORE
(EMPLOYEES, BOARD)

OUTER CORE
(CUSTOMERS, PARTNERS)

Generally, the order of importance and timeliness starts from the Inner Core and works outwards towards the Crust.

INTERNAL ALIGNMENT CHECK

When engaging with your various stakeholder levels, we use the acronym SAME.

S - Story (One consistent narrative)
A - Alignment (All teams on message)
M - Monitoring (What gets measured, gets managed)
E - Enforcement (Correct deviation)

It's critical that there's one consistent narrative and everyone is rowing in the same direction. If folks start going rogue, it'll take even the best-laid plan off track or, worse, tank it.

CONCLUSION

Understanding the anatomy of a crisis gives you a critical advantage, as it enables you to recognize patterns before they spiral out of control. Organizations that understand these patterns can intervene at the earliest stages, when the crisis is most manageable and before perceptions harden. Like our *Jurassic Park* example, those who pay attention to the ripples in the water glass can prepare before the T-Rex appears.

We've mapped the complete lifecycle of a crisis:

- The Early Warning System that identifies both external "meteors" and internal "time bombs"
- The distinct phases from Detective Mode through the Aftershocks
- The psychological responses that drive stakeholder behavior at each stage

But knowing what stage of a crisis you're facing is only the first step. The next critical decision is determining when to act and when to wait. Most organizations rush to respond immediately, often making situations worse through premature or poorly considered comments or actions. As we move into Chapter 3, we'll explore one of the most counterintuitive yet powerful tools in your crisis management arsenal: strategic silence. You'll learn when to speak, when to wait, and how to use a pause as an active strategy *rather* than a passive response.

CASE STUDY:
THE HIDDEN LETTER

Crisis Trigger: The biggest threat in a crisis isn't what you know, it's what you don't *yet* know. When a company discovered financial irregularities and a suddenly departing executive, they thought they were dealing with a straightforward embezzlement case. The early warning signs had appeared like ripples in water: Expenses growing more rapidly than usual, a key executive's unexpected resignation just before an audit, and the discovery of inadequate financial controls.

The Challenge: The board was furious upon discovering the executive had misappropriated company funds and was ready to launch an aggressive legal and PR campaign against the former executive, potentially triggering significant media coverage.

Strategic Approach: Before taking any public action, we conducted a thorough investigation that uncovered a hidden letter from the departed executive. Tucked away in a drawer was a letter penned by the former executive, which essentially said, "For every finger you point at me, three are pointing back at you." I'd never seen anything like it before. It was giving Evil Villain.

Implementation Challenges: The document meticulously detailed how the company's practices, board oversight failures, and culture had not only enabled but essentially encouraged financial misconduct. Going public would have created significantly greater reputational damage for the company than for the departed individual executive.

Resolution Path: When facing a situation where you're considering taking an aggressive public stance, first conduct a rigorous self-assessment.

We asked:

- What could the other side reveal about our practices or culture?
- What systemic issues might have contributed to this situation?
- What evidence might exist that could reframe the narrative against us?

Every once in a while, the wisest crisis response isn't the most aggressive one but rather the one that acknowledges shared responsibility and focuses on systemic improvement rather than individual blame. After the assessment, we had the company contact key stakeholders discreetly.

Lesson Learned: Before launching any crisis response, particularly one involving public accusations, organizations must thoroughly understand their own vulnerabilities and potential counterclaims that could emerge.

CHAPTER 3
THE POWER OF THE PAUSE

EXECUTIVE SUMMARY

Sometimes the most brilliant move is to say nothing...*yet.* Strategic silence isn't hiding or ignoring problems. It's buying time to get your facts straight and your strategy right before you speak.

Sometimes, the most powerful crisis response isn't an immediate statement but a strategic pause that allows for fact-gathering, team alignment, and message development. This chapter introduces the Active Silence Protocol, providing a framework for maintaining silence, using that time productively, and breaking your silence effectively when the moment is right. Through the Strategic Silence Decision Tree, you'll learn when to speak, when to wait, and how to confidently make those decisions even under intense pressure.

"This is a disaster! Eden, we need to get out in front and control the narrative."

The panicked voice of a Fortune-ranked executive belted through my phone at 3 AM. We were in vastly different time zones, but issues don't care what part of the world you're in. When running a multi-national company, things don't stay even remotely within your time zone. The company had just been accused of animal cruelty, and social media was starting to buzz. Legal hadn't even been briefed yet, but the PR team was already drafting statements. And here I was, about to tell the executive something he *definitely* didn't want to hear: "We need to wait."

STRATEGIC SILENCE AND TIMING

Here's what separates the pros from the amateurs in crisis management: Understanding that silence isn't surrender, it's strategy. Strategic silence isn't the same as ignoring a problem in hopes it'll blow over.

The moment a crisis hits, there's enormous pressure to react immediately. But here's what decades in Crisis PR have taught me: The most powerful move you can make is sometimes no move. At least, not yet. Think of it like a chess game. When you're in trouble, your instinct might be to move pieces as quickly as possible. But the best players? They take a breath. They assess the board. They think three moves ahead.

When used appropriately, strategic silence gives you narrative control. Narrative control doesn't mean that everyone will agree with you. For the majority of your opposers, you'll always be guilty no matter what proof you have to the contrary. Haters gonna hate. (Or, as my favorite holiday shirt with Beaker on it says, "Meepers gonna meep.[2]")

How Strategic Silence Gives You Narrative Control:

- Prevention of missteps
- Time to gather facts
- Space for emotions to cool
- Team alignment opportunity

BEING QUICK IS GOOD. BUT IT'S A DOUBLE-EDGED SWORD.

The upside: You want to be first because whoever is out front sets the tone of the story and the terms of what's being discussed. You're in the driver's seat. Your audience will look to you as the arbiter of what's legitimate and what's not.

The downside: Whoever is in front runs the risk of getting ahead of the facts and stumbling. You lose credibility if you have to backpedal to correct or "clarify" mistakes. Without credibility, you lose trust. Without trust, you lose. Don't turn into *The Boy Who Cried Wolf.*

The lesson: Make sure your facts are as solid as possible. If they're uncertain, paint a vivid and convincing picture of what you do know. Then, let people's imaginations run with it.

THINK BEFORE YOU SPEAK OR POST ONLINE

You need to think before you speak and choose your words with the precision of a surgeon.

Faced with unexpected and unwanted situations, clients too often are inclined to blurt out the first thing that comes to mind. You gotta say something, and you gotta say it now, right?

Only half right. You do have to say something. But it must be thoughtful. It must be calibrated to project the right message and tone. It mustn't undercut your defenses with an unintended hint of culpability or whiff of uncertainty.

The other half is wrong. It's rare that you must respond in the moment. (Hello again, Strategic Silence!) It's also unwise unless you know beforehand what will be asked and your comments are carefully scripted.

Usually, you can buy time. The more, the better. But don't take too long, or it looks like you've "gone silent." That makes you seem guilty.

But wait…what's the difference between a "strategic silence" and "gone silent"?!? I'm glad you asked.

Is an insistent reporter poking a microphone in your face and demanding you answer his questions? Politely say, "Let me check on that, and I'll get back to you." Keep your promise.

Is the media on the phone? Have your assistant screen the calls. Learn why the journalist is calling *(he'll share that)*, and what his specific questions are *(he'll withhold the juiciest and most important)*, what his deadline is *(he'll always tell you it's sooner than it really is)*.

Immediately call your Crisis PR strategist. What are the facts? What should you say? What will have the desired effect on your reputation? What's legally permissible?

Then, get back to the reporter <u>before</u> his deadline. By what means?

A phone call is more personal, but there's a danger that the journalist will steer the conversation into undesired terrain.

Email is more formal. That's good and bad. Good because you have a record of what you said. Bad because a record exists (especially if, in retrospect, you wish you hadn't said it).

Next time the media approaches you, ask: What will allow you to control the conversation and steer it where you want it to go?

So, what about social media? It doesn't have deadlines like reporters. While the timeline for how long you can go without posting something has shrunk and highly depends on the situation, you sometimes have less than a day to get something up, especially if your audience is accustomed to hearing from your company multiple times a day. (*Major caveat:* If you're in the middle of a crisis, you should suspend any regularly scheduled posts until the situation is under control. Otherwise, it'll look tone-deaf.)

For social media, it essentially comes down to not posting something just for the sake of posting. Your first post sets the tone for how your audience and the public react to any further updates. If you post something hastily before considering the what and why, you'll risk making the situation worse than if you held off for a few more hours…maaaaybe a whole day, if you're lucky.

THE ACTIVE SILENCE PROTOCOL

The value of this approach will become even more evident when we examine the breastfeeding backlash case study at the end of this chapter. There, you'll see how a luxury retailer's decision to pause, assess, and strategize instead of immediately issuing a defensive statement transformed what could have been a public relations disaster into a contained and quickly resolved situation.

Being strategically silent doesn't mean being passive; it means being deliberate. Here's your action plan:

Internal Alignment:

- Brief leadership
- Align messaging
- Establish protocols (these should largely already be in place)
- Prep frontline staff

External Preparation:

- Draft responses for various stakeholders (consistent core messaging that's tailored to each group's interests)
- Prep spokespeople (always have a backup person in case your main spokesperson is unavailable)
- Develop any assets, if necessary (official general statement, press release, special website or dedicated area on site, informational packets, hotlines, etc.)

Monitoring & Analysis:

- Track social sentiment
- Monitor media coverage
- Analyze stakeholder reactions
- Identify emerging narratives

THE SCIENCE OF TIMING

This isn't a science per se, it's more like alchemy. Depending on the information you have and the timing of that info, the if/when/how you approach a situation will change.

At the base level, you must assemble your team and conduct an initial assessment. You must also lock down communication: speculating openly outside the team is a no-no.

From there, you need to gather relevant information quickly and accurately. The information you gather will inform how you proceed with developing your strategy. This is why, when someone comes up to me at a party, pitches me for 20 seconds, and then expects me to tell them how to fix it, I shoot back some version of, "It might cause more harm than good to offer advice given that I know so little about the situation."

HOW DO I KNOW WHICH STRATEGY TO USE?

Is a problem brewing on the horizon? You must deal with it before it festers. Some clients get it instantly. They want to be prepared to avoid likely disturbances in the force. (Yes, a *Star Wars* reference.)

The best time to do damage control is *before* damage happens. Do it well, and as far as the rest of the world knows, it never happened. You don't need to be clairvoyant to achieve this. Trust your gut. If it tells you something's wrong, it probably is.

A company knew major operational changes were in the pipeline and prepared in advance to cushion the impact. It recognized that people instinctively resisted change and feared it might cause an exodus of worried employees, especially managers in whom it had a lot invested. We rolled out the changes in a non-threatening manner and motivated employees to embrace them. This included articles from executives on their intranet and in newsletters about their excitement or the company's future. In the end, we exceeded expectations. There was no exodus, and normal attrition decreased by 50%.

Wise enough to take control early on? You wish that nothing bad comes out, but you're prepared for it in case it does. As a result, you can quickly turn the situation around and make it a short-lived story.

A resident at a celebrity rehab center was abusing and endangering other residents and staff. The facility was facing a backlash from other residents, the media, and the community. We anticipated the shape and tone of the dispute and crafted letters and a Q&A to make it clear that management had fixed the problem and that the facility was safe. In addition, we prepared a crisis plan that has become their gold standard. Ultimately, it was short-lived since the story was not fueled by information coming out in dribs and drabs, or was primarily based on speculation. One news cycle, and it was over. Also, none of the other residents left.

Forced to be reactive? Beware of absolute denials; select your words carefully based on the facts. Can you be proactive? Shift the burden to your accuser; make them prove the allegations. What's the status of your company's credibility and reputation? Does it need protection or redemption?

A student at a child-care center was accused of bullying another child. The mother threatened to sue and generated a flurry of media attention. The police and state licensing agency began investigations. The situation was evolving quickly. Our strategy was to anticipate developments. We crafted a statement to the media and letters to the parents and government funding agencies. We created scripts for 1-on-1 follow-up calls to parents. The goal of all the communications was to reassure and comfort. As a result, reassurances soothed nervousness. No parents removed their children. Government funds weren't interrupted. Investigations cleared the center, and the media fell silent. The matter was soon forgotten.

Are you currently in the storm? If the media is involved, there are two possible outcomes.

First, the negative story never appears (a.k.a. "sidetracking" or "killing" a story). This is perhaps the greatest challenge for the Crisis PR strategist. To succeed, you must stop it before the reporter invests significant time and before it's been pre-sold to the editor. Once either of those happens, a story assumes a life of its own, and inertia takes over.

This requires the most nuanced work with the media. No room for clumsy actions or ill-chosen words. What strategies will resonate with the media? Can you offer the reporter a more appealing story? How do you do it without offending or making him suspect he's onto something hot?

It's not enough to just ask yourself these questions. You must know the answers and act quickly.

A prominent organization was going to implement a series of changes and brought us in early, hoping to avoid a spectacle. We found a positive angle that deflected the media's inclination to seek "the real back story." As a result, few media carried the story, and those that did were perfunctory or positive. All equally desirable.

Second, pivoting and shifting the spotlight. This is used if a story can't be stopped. The good news is that you have tools to make it less bad. Which to use depends on what was done, how public the issue's become, and how badly your reputation has been injured.

Are you trying to pick up the pieces after the storm? The worst outcome is when you're already pummeled before you seek help. The damage to your reputation is deep, and the tide is flowing against you. Cleaning up a mess after the fact is a form of triage, and that's always more intensive and time-consuming. Your options are limited, and the cost is often several times higher.

Warning: If the news cycle has long passed and the dust has settled, don't kick it up and create a reason for journalists to start a new news cycle.

A bank botched the process of firing its CEO and COO, sparking a media firestorm. We were brought in to clean up the mess. The media was planning a follow-up story based on speculation, and we stopped that in its tracks by offering something they wanted even more: a sit-down interview with the Chairman if they'd hold off for 24 hours. We used the time to script the interview to shift the spotlight. As a result, the initial negative coverage was quickly replaced with positive stories about the bank's vision for the future.

THE STRATEGIC SILENCE DECISION TREE

The Strategic Silence Decision Tree guides organizations through a systematic evaluation process before taking communicative action. It consists of three major phases, each with four critical checkpoints that must be satisfied before proceeding.

The process begins with Information Assessment, where you first verify all facts about the situation. This means having concrete evidence and documentation to support your understanding. Once facts are verified, you assess whether you fully understand the scope of the situation: its boundaries, limitations, and potential reach. Next, you map out all possible impacts across different stakeholder groups and scenarios. Finally, you ensure responses are prepared for various potential outcomes and questions.

Moving into the Readiness Check phase, you first confirm that all team members are aligned on the approach and understand their roles. Then, you verify that the necessary resources (human, financial, or technical) are in place. Message testing follows, ensuring that your communications have been evaluated for their relevance to target audiences. The phase concludes with a systems check to confirm that all technical and operational components are functioning properly.

The final Timing Evaluation phase is crucial for optimal impact. It starts with an assessment of the current news cycle to ensure your message won't be lost or misinterpreted amid other major stories. You then confirm all stakeholders are prepared for the communication. The third checkpoint assesses whether you have garnered the necessary attention from your target audience. The final check confirms you have established sufficient control over the narrative and messaging environment.

A "no" answer triggers a pause or wait state at each checkpoint, preventing progression until that specific criterion is met. This ensures a methodical, thorough approach to strategic communication decisions.

This decision framework complements the Strategic Response Framework examined in Chapter 1 and the crisis stages timeline presented in Chapter 2. Together, these tools determine when to gather more information, maintain strategic silence, and break that silence with a carefully constructed response. In Chapter 4, we'll build on this foundation by exploring how to craft strategic narratives once you've determined it's time to communicate.

INFORMATION ASSESSMENT

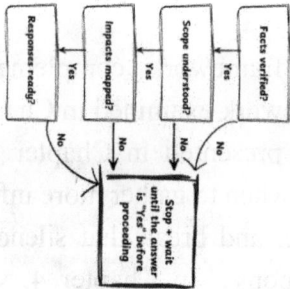

Facts verified? → Yes → Scope understood? → Yes → Impacts mapped? → Yes → Responses ready?

No → Stop + wait until the answer is "Yes" before proceeding

READINESS CHECK

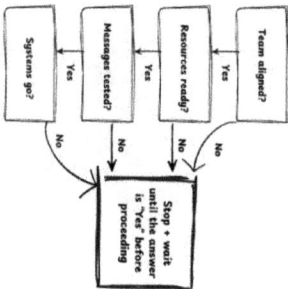

Team aligned? → Yes → Resources ready? → Yes → Messages tested? → Yes → Systems go?

No → Stop + wait until the answer is "Yes" before proceeding

TIMING EVALUATION

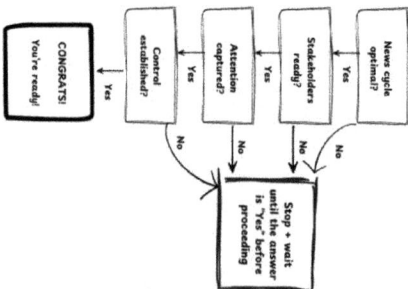

News cycle optimal? → Yes → Stakeholders ready? → Yes → Attention captured? → Yes → Control established? → Yes → CONGRATS! You're ready!

No → Stop + wait until the answer is "Yes" before proceeding

BREAKING YOUR SILENCE

When you <u>do</u> speak, make it count. Your response should be:

- **Clear and confident:** During chaotic, uncertain, or emotional times, clarity helps eliminate confusion. The fewer words, the better. Your delivery also needs to have confidence. If you seem unsure of yourself, then why should you expect others to feel confident in what you're saying?
- **Fact-based:** Inaccurate information tanks your credibility, either by insisting that something never happened or happened very differently when others can see the facts clearly. Repeating a lie won't magically make it true. Think of a little boy asked by his Mother about cookies that disappeared from the cookie jar. Or the Emperor in Hans Christian Andersen's *The Emperor's New Clothes*. The same applies to companies.
- **Aligned with your values:** You can't say one thing and then do another. If you're paying lip service without backing it up with actions that are aligned with what you said, the internet will come for you.
- **Forward-looking:** You want to shift the spotlight and not dwell on it.
- **Action-oriented:** What are you doing to ensure this never happens again? Be careful with this, though. If you can't ensure it won't happen again, it's better to under-promise (a.k.a. lower the risk of a repeat). This is especially true when elements are beyond your control (i.e., regulations, government, environment, etc.).

Here's what this looks like in practice:

Layer 1: The Critical First Minutes

(The moment when everyone's watching)

Picture this: It's 9:47 AM when the crisis breaks. Your phone is blowing up, social media is on fire, and everyone's waiting for your response. This is where most leaders stumble, but here's what winning looks like:

Initial Response Elements:

- **Acknowledge:** "We are aware of the situation with [issue]"
- **Understand:** "We recognize the impact this has on [stakeholders]"
- **Own It:** "As CEO, I take full responsibility"
- **Act:** "Here are the immediate steps we're taking..."

Layer 2: The First Hours

(When you need to back up words with action)

This is where you prove your first statement wasn't just talk. You need:

- Verifiable facts (not just reassurances)
- Clear timeline of events and actions (it doesn't need to be exhaustive)
- Specific steps being taken (for the public, this also doesn't need to be exhaustive)
- Concrete resources being deployed (optional)

Layer 3: The Path Forward

(Showing this won't happen again)

This is your chance to turn crisis into opportunity by outlining (some, not all, are necessary):

- Systemic solutions
- Prevention strategies
- Process improvements
- Long-term commitments

THE FOUR Cs: YOUR COMMUNICATION COMPASS

While leadership requires the Three Cs we just discussed, your actual communications should follow the Four Cs as your compass. Many leaders get lost here because they have the structure but miss the substance. Think of the following as your guiding lights:

Clarity means stripping out jargon and speaking plainly. Instead of saying, "We are implementing enhanced procedural protocols," say, "We're adding three new safety checks." When that tech company faced its data breach, its CEO kept it simple: "We were hacked. Customer data was taken. Here's what we're doing about it." Not corporate wallpaper. Just the truth.

Consistency ensures your message is recognizable across every touchpoint (emails to employees, social media posts, press statements, etc.) Think of it like a song where the words might shift slightly, but the melody (your core message) stays the same.

Compassion isn't about legal liability; it's about recognizing the human impact. Demonstrate that you understand the concern, acknowledge the frustration, and feel the disappointment. Express your commitment to making it right. (Caveat: You shouldn't say something your attorney thinks will likely open you up to legal liability.)

Finally, **Credibility** comes from backing every statement with substance: verified facts, concrete actions, clear processes, and regular updates. It's not just what you say, it's what you prove.

COMMON PITFALLS TO AVOID

The Template Trap Don't just fill in blanks in a pre-written statement. While the framework is consistent, your response must feel authentic to your situation.

The Kitchen Sink Don't try to address everything at once. Layer your response like a well-planned meal, not an all-you-can-eat cruise buffet.

The Pivot Too Soon Don't rush to the "moving forward" message before properly addressing the current situation. You have to go through the pain before you can talk about the gain.

Remember: Each crisis is unique, but this framework remains constant. Think of this framework as a trusted map, not a template or exact formula. The terrain will always be different, but the landmarks that guide you home remain the same. The art is adapting it to your specific situation while maintaining its core integrity.

WHEN THERE'S AN INFORMATION VOID, THE INTERNET WILL FILL IT

In life, timeliness is essential. Miss the window, and you're S.O.L.

In business: Inventing a product before the market is ready. In dating: "It's meeting the man of my dreams and then meeting his beautiful wife. (And isn't it ironic? Don't you think?)"[3]

Or in the media: Getting your story published 10 minutes after your arch-nemesis makes headlines with their version of the same story.

The genesis of an article was a sexy sound bite from Chattanooga's mayor saying there'd been a "horrific incident" involving a shooting and a military site. Nothing else was known.

Even the New York Times dispatched two reporters hot on the trail of the story.

Why? Because the media was ultra-sensitized. It wasn't long after a South Carolina church massacre that caused the Deep South to reconsider its allegiance to Civil War symbols. And it was on the same day as a jury was deliberating over a movie theater massacre in Colorado.

What resulted?

The media cobbled together bits and pieces from a lot of loosely related people, essentially saying they had no idea what happened. The same happened about a week later after a theater shooting in Louisiana.

This is how misinformation gets pumped into the rumor mill.

Getting out in front of your audience and telling your story is essential. In public matters, it's up to the civil authorities to get the facts out. But what about when it's at your company or on your property?

Like a sample sale in Manhattan in the early 2000s, you need to move quickly and decisively. Then the onus is on you. No time for delay or uncertainty. You must have someone on the scene immediately (figuratively or literally) armed with facts and the authority to speak. Don't stick your foot in your mouth or leave your audience with more questions than they arrived with.

When there's an absence of facts, reporters will fill the void with what's at hand. Usually, that's speculation.

CONCLUSION

Strategic silence isn't the absence of action. Strategic Silence is a deliberate approach that gives you control over the narrative when it matters most. As we've seen throughout this chapter, knowing when and how to pause can differentiate between a manageable situation and a full-blown crisis.

We've explored:

- How strategic silence provides the time to gather facts, align your team, and develop a comprehensive response
- The Active Silence Protocol that transforms waiting into a strategic advantage
- The Decision Tree that guides when to maintain silence and when to break it
- The critical elements of breaking your silence effectively when the time is right

Remember that CEO who was awakened at 3 AM with demands for an immediate statement? They transformed a potential disaster into a manageable situation by implementing strategic silence. The organization didn't appear unresponsive. Instead, they appeared thoughtful, deliberate, and in control.

In Chapter 4, we'll build on this foundation of strategic timing to explore how to construct powerful narratives that shape perception in your favor. Because when you *do* break your silence, what you say and how you say it will determine whether you merely survive the crisis or emerge stronger on the other side.

CASE STUDY:
THE BREASTFEEDING BACKLASH

The principles of strategic silence we've explored throughout this chapter aren't just theoretical, they're practical tools that can transform potential PR disasters into manageable situations. The following case study illustrates how the Active Silence Protocol, when properly implemented, enabled a luxury retailer to gather crucial information, develop an effective strategy, and control the narrative during what could have been a devastating social media backlash. Note how strategic silence wasn't passive waiting but rather active preparation that created the foundation for a successful response.

Crisis Trigger

A luxury retailer faced a rapidly escalating social media crisis after a new mother began breastfeeding in their high-end store. A store manager politely informed her that she was visible on security cameras and offered a more private lounge area if she preferred. The mother initially seemed fine with this interaction and continued shopping happily for another hour. However, upon leaving, she immediately took to the internet, claiming she had been illegally discouraged and bullied for breastfeeding. Within hours, the "mommy-sphere" was in uproar across social platforms. The story spread through mommy blogs, Facebook groups, and Twitter, with calls for a well-publicized "nurse-in" protest at the store. (Yes, a time before TikTok.)

Initial Response

When I received the call from the panicked store owner, they were already drafting a defensive statement explaining store policy and citing security concerns. My first move was to halt this approach, which would have poured fuel on the fire. Instead, we implemented our Active Silence

Protocol to gain critical time for investigation:

- We assembled a small crisis team, including the store owner, the manager involved in the incident, their attorney, and me.
- We quickly interviewed everyone involved, documenting their recollections while memories were fresh.
- We reviewed security footage to verify precisely what had occurred.
- We identified the key online communities where the story was spreading.
- We also did a little background research on the accuser.

This investigation revealed crucial facts: the interaction had been brief and professional, the mother had shown no signs of distress at the time, store employees had continued to provide standard customer service throughout her visit, and the woman had a history of extorting businesses in the area.

Strategic Approach

Rather than issuing a broad public statement that might amplify the situation, we developed a targeted multi-channel strategy:

- **Narrative Architecture**: We crafted a factual narrative acknowledging the mother's right to breastfeed while providing context about the store's family-friendly policies and the simple offer of an optional private space
- **Stakeholder Mapping**: We identified three key groups to address:

  - The direct accuser and her immediate circle
  - Influential voices in the mommy-blogger community
  - General customers concerned about the store's values

- **Platform-Specific Approach**:

  - For public platforms (Yelp, Facebook): Brief, factual corrections focused on store policies encased in our empathetic approach
  - For private channels: More detailed explanations with the mommy-blogger influencers
  - For media inquiries: Prepared statement and talking points emphasizing family-friendly values

- **Legal Coordination**: We worked with legal counsel to ensure all communications acknowledged breastfeeding rights while accurately representing what had occurred

Implementation Challenges

Several factors complicated our implementation:

- **Emotional Intensity**: The issue touched on deeply personal parental rights and identity, creating high emotional stakes
- **Coordinated Opposition**: Several activist groups had joined the conversation, seeing an opportunity to advance broader causes
- **Media Interest**: Local news outlets began calling for interviews about the "controversy"
- **Internal Concern**: Store employees worried about being portrayed as insensitive or discriminatory

Resolution Path

Our implementation proceeded through three distinct phases:

Phase 1: Direct Engagement

- We posted a factual, empathetic response directly to the accuser's public Yelp review
- We reached out privately to three key mommy-blogger influencers who were driving much of the conversation

- We provided these influencers with additional context and our security footage policies (not the actual footage)

Phase 2: Community Outreach

- We identified and engaged supportive voices within the mommy community
- We shared more detailed information about the store's history of accommodating families
- We highlighted testimonials from other mothers who had positive experiences

Phase 3: Media Management

- When the media began calling, we directed them to our public responses
- We emphasized the private, personalized nature of the resolution process
- We declined on-camera interviews that might reignite the situation (and because the owner was still shaken up about the entire situation and was not camera-ready)

Outcome Analysis

- No news stories ever ran about the incident because journalists found no controversy once they reviewed the facts
- The original accuser posted a follow-up acknowledging it had been a "misunderstanding" and removed her negative reviews

- Several initial critics actually became customers after learning more about the store's family-friendly approach
- The planned "nurse-in" protest never materialized as support dissipated

From crisis to resolution, it took only 36 hours, with minimal business disruption and no lasting damage to the reputation.

Lessons Learned

This case illustrates several key principles:

- **Speed vs. Strategy**: Taking time to gather facts before responding publicly prevented escalation
- **Direct Engagement**: Addressing concerns at their source prevented wider spread
- **Platform Specificity**: Using different approaches for different channels maximized effectiveness
- **Narrative Control**: By focusing on facts rather than defensiveness, we shaped a more accurate and positive perception
- **Community Dynamics**: Understanding and working within the social dynamics of the mommy community was crucial to the resolution

CHAPTER 4
STRATEGIC NARRATIVE
ARCHITECTURE

EXECUTIVE SUMMARY

The narrative people believe about your crisis matters more than what actually happened. Build that story intentionally.

In any crisis, multiple versions of the truth compete for acceptance. This chapter teaches you how to make your version the one that sticks through strategic narrative architecture. You'll learn how to control the facts to control the story, navigate the spectrum of narrative control from stopping stories to generating them, and leverage Litigation PR to tell your story on your terms. Through the Multi-Platform Protocol and the Known-Unknown Framework, you'll develop the skills to maintain consistency while adapting your approach to different communication channels. Most importantly, you'll master the three-phase Narrative Evolution that transforms crisis response from reactive damage control into strategic storytelling.

In any crisis, multiple versions of the truth are floating around. Your job isn't just to tell your version, it's to make yours the version that sticks. Think of it like a building: you need a solid foundation (your core truth), strong walls (your supporting evidence), and a roof that protects everything (your strategic messaging).

There's an old adage in Crisis PR: "Lose focus, and you lose control. Lose control, and you lose."

There's a big difference between being in control versus being controlling. The same applies to guiding perception versus being manipulative. The first ones have a positive connotation, the latter have a negative connotation.

Is there a difference in reality?

Sometimes, sometimes not. But only one measure truly matters: Are you achieving your goal? If so, you're doing your job right. It has nothing to do with being nice or not. It has everything to do with being effective. You must control the situation, or it will control you.

It doesn't matter whether your audience is your employees, consumers, community groups, a court of law, or the court of public opinion.

Defining tone matters. When you do, all else follows:

Whether the image created is positive or negative. Whether the language is reasonable or shrill. Whether the public shrugs and moves on, or feels compelled to pick sides.

A nasty and protracted dispute was settled and needed to be announced publicly. We volunteered to draft a joint statement, and the CEO agreed immediately: "It's a basic lesson from first-year law school: If you do the drafting, you get 70% of what you want."

We got 95%.

CONTROL THE FACTS. CONTROL THE STORY.

In Crisis & Reputation Management, when the worst occurs, you don't try to wish the bad away by ignoring it. You take control. Analyze your options.

What has the other side done and what'll they do next?

What does the media know and what might they find out? How can you create the advantage by going on offense or shifting a negative to your benefit?

You stay focused. If possible, keep the issue below the public's radar. If not, have a backup plan and be prepped. Better to have a strategy in place and not need it, than to need it and not have one.

The media is hungry for solid information. What does the media want? What does it need?

What should you say and not say? Have you identified those qualified and authorized to speak to the media and those who aren't? How do you respond immediately (when necessary) and delay (when possible)? How do you short-circuit rumors and speculation? How do you deal with antagonistic reporters and cultivate those who are neutral?

If you're quick and credible, you can feed necessary morsels. You're setting the tone and shaping the story to lessen the damage to your business and reputation.

This also gives you an opportunity to intercept errors before they become public. After mistakes are in the public domain, they take on a life of their own and are much harder to fix. That's why it's critical to know in advance what to do and not do in fast-moving situations.

Nothing is more important than protecting your reputation. Because Reputation Is Your Most Valuable Asset®

Is outrageous behavior by celebrities acceptable, if the same would land you in jail? Are sexual indiscretions by politicians abhorrent when a political opponent commits them, but excusable when your party does? Is the NSA's data collection keeping you safe or intruding on your personal space? Are rising temperatures in one period incontrovertible evidence of a coming cataclysm, but stable or falling temperatures in a subsequent period just a statistical blip? Is military action OK if you feel threatened and do it, but evil when an enemy does?

The winner is whoever defines the debate: the words used to describe, the images conjured, the emotions evoked.

We see the results whenever we open a newspaper, turn on the TV, or read a story online. The person controlling the strings is usually unseen. They work behind the scenes to shape what you see and hear.

The public starts with a bias against business. Distrust and suspicion are the default. Non-profits are usually given the benefit of the doubt. However, they're held to a higher standard, making it easier for them to trip up.

Clients find themselves in undesirable situations every day. They land in litigation. Government investigators come knocking at the door. Funds are embezzled or mismanaged. Harassment or abuse occurs. Labor issues get nasty.

When is the best time to begin erecting defenses? As soon as you become aware of a potential problem, and before it becomes public.

The worst time is after you're already in a negative spotlight. At that point, you're on defense, and your options are limited.

What's it they say about the early bird and the worm? There's a reason why that's a truism.

MULTI-PLATFORM PROTOCOL

Social media has turned crisis communications into a 24/7 high-wire act. You're not just managing traditional media anymore, you're conducting an orchestra of tweets, posts, shares, and comments, all while walking that wire. We'll explore detailed platform-specific strategies in Chapter 5.

The Multi-Platform Protocol:

- Responsive, but not reactive (strategy before action)
- Fast, but not rushed (verify before posting)

- Present, but not overwhelming (quality over quantity)
- Consistent, but not robotic (human touch matters)

Think of it like Doctor Strange using the Time Stone in Marvel's *Infinity War*. You need to see all possible futures before you make your move. One wrong post can create a thousand alternate timelines, and none of them are good.

Because of the speed at which things move, you must be extra cautious. You were outta luck the moment you posted it.

Take a moment to think before posting or publishing anything online. You can't hit "Undo" and bring the boo-boo back. Someone might have already taken a screenshot. Maybe you can make it less bad, but you can never make it unhappen.

Back in the good old days of traditional media, executives' greatest nightmares were some publications with a small, local reach or classic word-of-mouth. Yes, it could harm the business, but relatively, you'd survive.

Now, folks are Googling "How to respond to social media attacks" while their phones continue to ping with new notifications.

It's not only what you type or post that poses potential problems. Beware of what you say or do offline. People whip out their phones and start recording almost instinctively nowadays. In a heartbeat, an embarrassing or legally problematic video of you could be trending online.

When social media's rage strikes, it can be swift, and you're going to wish you had the expertise of crisis managers in your team!

It can feel completely overwhelming and get messy really quickly if not handled correctly.

Imagine watching a video of one of your favorite restaurants' food with a side of bugs.

The business owners were panicking, and social media's power wasn't in their favor. Almost as soon as the short, 10-second video went viral, we were called in to manage the message.

Another company came under fire for what the public thought was poor product placement.

A show had used one of the company's products in a scene that ultimately didn't sit well with the Twitterverse. It wasn't the company's fault, but it got dragged into the spotlight and was forced to defend itself. The Director of Communications & Marketing called us in a panic. They had no idea how to respond. (I know what you're thinking, but it's not Peloton's seemingly never-ending saga with 'And Just Like That'. This situation is way more common than you think!)

We've watched companies go bankrupt after responding poorly during a social media attack that left lasting damage. But some businesses survive these storms and actually THRIVE after them.

"How?!?" you ask. Here's our secret:

NARRATIVE CONTROL

We've developed a narrative control framework that turns a media crisis, whether traditional or social media, to your advantage.

Here are 4 of the steps in our framework:

Figure Out Facts

Unleash your inner Sherlock Holmes and focus on the critical questions rather than worrying. What actually happened? Who's alleging what and why? Is there proof that what they're saying is true? Do they have a motive to attack us? Do we need to launch a formal investigation? Don't let the list of questions racing through your head cause you to freeze. Stop panicking and start planning! It's time to gather your crisis team and make some magic happen. Be as fast as the social media wind and begin connecting the dots with your team.

Identify Your Audience

Don't feel compelled to use all the platforms available. Focus on the one or two most important to you and your target audience.

Be strategic about your next move and focus on reaching your target audience in one strike. For social media, it may be the source of the post, the group that's impacted, or the media's social media account. For traditional media, this includes which publications you want to target. You may care more about the online group, local paper, or trade publication in tight-knit communities. Often, the best solution is to go after the big fish: the one that will set the tone. It's the big fish that smaller publications or other accounts will take their lead from and run similar stories.

Craft Your Message

Reassurance and trust are essential for human beings to de-escalate and re-evaluate a situation. Rely on the three R's:

Reassure. Reassure. Reassure.

Live in your audience's mind. What are they feeling right now? Are they devastated, angry, or confused? Reassure them! Show them that you care, and, more importantly, take action.

Post It

The majority of the strategizing and intensity of the situation are over. However, this doesn't mean you should lose momentum and walk away. To be effective, you need to monitor how your message was received and respond accordingly.

You're in a much stronger position by partnering with your crisis team to handle the situation. Their outside perspective and deep knowledge of handling situations similar to yours can't be replicated.

(For additional thoughts from Eden on how to make a social media apology, check out the Inc Magazine article "4 Steps for Creating an Authentic Video Apology"[4].)

THE SPECTRUM OF NARRATIVE CONTROL

Stopping a story from being published. If you want to stop a story before it's published, you need to nip it in the bud.

A large non-profit was being investigated by a federal agency. A major news organization had gotten a whiff and was snooping around. The client was terrified that the issue might become public and that their dirty laundry would be aired for the world to see. We succeeded in sidetracking the story. First, by assuring the reporter that it wasn't competitive and no other news outlets were pursuing it. This relieved the urgency. Finally, by cutting a deal with reporter, we agreed that if an investigation were conducted and any wrongdoing were found, we'd grant her the complete access she desired. In exchange, she agreed to write nothing until that time. As a result, the reporter held off on writing a story until we were ready to release the whole picture. A rare occurrence in today's world.

Epilogue: Six months later, a separate problem arose, and the client's lawyer urged that we be brought back because we'd protected them so successfully before. But the client refused, complaining that we "didn't even break a sweat." Within days, the client was pilloried in the media.

Sadly, that's the downside to doing a job so well that you make it look easy.

Avoiding hit pieces. If you're successful in life, you risk making someone jealous or upsetting your market or niche. These personal rivals and professional competitors would love to see you get your comeuppance and would be happy to help the media build a "hit piece" against you. Sometimes, it may even be a disgruntled current or former employee.

(For additional thoughts from Eden, check out her Inc Magazine article "How to Minimize Brand Damage When Disgruntled Employees Stir the Pot"[5].)

A chief executive was warned that his company might be the target of a negative story in a respected industry publication. A board member told the CEO to call us and get prepared for the worst. The hit piece was likely, but it wasn't certain. So we couldn't prematurely pop our heads out of the foxhole without creating a story if there wasn't one. Instead, we crafted a strong argument as to why the allegations were untrue, and we prepped the client so he'd be armed if the call came. Setting the tone was critical. The CEO mustn't be argumentative because that resolves little. The goal was to gently convince the reporter that he was acting on bad information and that publishing it could damage his reputation as a reliable journalist. As a result, the journalist didn't want to take the chance of ruining their own reputation, so the story never got published.

Handling a hit piece. First, find out what the reporter thinks he knows and whether the allegations are true or not.

If they're untrue: Crisis PR strategists can reach out to the reporter on an off-the-record basis and provide context and background. If successful, the story can be sidetracked.

If they're true: You've got some explaining to do. If the reporter wants to talk to someone, figure out who's the best person for the job. This decision is highly strategic. It determines not only who the "face" is but how much access you want to give the media. Will the Crisis PR strategist speak on behalf of the company? Will the internal PR person? Will the CEO himself?

Softening or refocusing a story. If you can't stop a story from being published, don't fret. You have options.

Some routine (but threatening-sounding) paperwork needed to be filed, so a subordinate did it without checking who was affected. One was a popular nightspot with a large and vocal following. The reaction was fast and furious. It became a *cause célèbre* on Facebook and Instagram and in news outlets large and small. It was a misunderstanding of what was actually happening. Could it have been handled better? Yes, and it should have. That may have avoided the problem in the first place. But that ship had sailed. Now, we needed to turn it around. That meant clarifying the context, explaining what it really meant, and reassuring the public that their beloved nightspot wasn't in imminent peril. We identified and contacted all key influencers. Next, we saved our most powerful stuff for the most influential news organization. After selling it on a storyline that shifted the tone, other media followed suit. Throughout it all, only the client was visible. We provided the strategy and polished the message, but remained unseen lest the public wonder why we were needed. As a result, after we got involved, the issue quickly went away.

Turning the tables with the media. Shift the burden and make the other side prove their allegations. How? You must redefine the nature of the story. Sell your version to the most influential news organization covering the issue. Why would they buy it? Because what you offer gives the reporter an edge over his rivals: insight that gives his story more depth or an angle nobody else has.

The rest will follow suit. The herd instinct is strong in the media. Other reporters will try to get back out in front themselves. This is an opportunity. You'll control the story if you can feed this competition.

A case involving alleged misuse of corporate funds on a large scale had taken on a life of its own. We were brought in late. The government already had solid control of the media. We selected a reporter from a national publication, promised him access to the client, and laid out our story. We never expected the underlying allegations to go away. But we got the client a fair hearing, which shifted the tone of coverage for all media going forward.

A non-profit foundation was pounded by allegations from a few disgruntled former employees. It was major news for the local media, and they were having a field day chasing the rumors *du jour*. What did we do? Took the story to the state's biggest paper, which hadn't been covering it at all and would likely cover it only once. In the end, it was exactly as expected. The reporter's first (and only) article examined the situation unencumbered by local passions. Of course, the allegations had to be part of the story. But so were denials by the client and, more importantly, refutations by government agencies. All in all, the client fared well, and the allegations came across as spurious. Soon, the story disappeared, even in the local media.

Generating a story. Sometimes, it's to your benefit to create media attention. This is especially true in litigation, where the goal is to persuade the opposing side to settle.

Warning: Two can play this game. If you think there's a chance the other side will try to do this, you need to beat them to the punch.

A prominent entertainer and golfer was in a dispute with a businessman who owned a private golf club. Not much money was involved. But for the entertainer, it was the principle. So he filed suit. We worked with his attorney before filing to be fully prepared to hit the ground running when the suit was issued. We crafted a story for the press that would make it hard for them to pass up. As a result, we achieved extensive media coverage that shined a harsh light on the other side. Within hours after the story was published, the businessman called the manager of his golf club with a simple order: "Settle this, immediately."

Getting the other side to settle. Ultimately, your goal is to win. How you get there is less important than what you achieve. Sometimes, the most effective path is litigation.

A legendary rock band was embroiled in a trademark dispute with a cable network but couldn't get traction. We took the fight public. Litigation was filed, and we generated worldwide news coverage that left the cable network red-faced. The result was a quick and favorable out-of-court settlement for our client. But not all disputes need to (or should) be litigated, or are on the media's radar.

When two co-owners created a clothing company, they were in sync. New dynamics emerged as their fashions became all the rage among the tween set. One owner insisted that if the company focused only on design, it would run itself. The other recognized the need to start acting like a real enterprise with scores of employees and revenues well into seven figures. Splitting duties between the creative and business sides had worked well...until it didn't. Bitter internal struggles erupted over which "side" wielded ultimate decision-making power. Our role was to listen and act as the voice of reason for our client (one of the co-owners). We steered strategy and communications to ensure our client's voice was heard and understood. In the end, our client received what they felt they deserved in the partnership, and a newfound balance was restored within the clothing company.

LEVERAGING LITIGATION PR

"That's not nice!" the young assistant frowned after reviewing a storyline being pitched to the media about a nasty lawsuit.

"That's not the point," his boss explained calmly. "Our job isn't to make the other side feel good. It's to make sure our client wins in the public's perception."

Litigation PR, where the goal is to create pain for the other side to make them see the wisdom of settling, is the flip side of Crisis Management, where the goal is to protect a client's reputation from damage.

Why file suit? Because that's the battlefield on which disputes are frequently fought. Reporters tend to give more credence to arguments made in litigation.

Before filing a legal complaint, your lawyer should think about what would benefit you in a court of law <u>and</u> in the court of public opinion. You're not just making legal arguments. You're telling your story on your terms to alter public perception.

How to do it? Strategically insert language into legal filings to make allegations, clarify events, and redefine rationale and goals to cast the client in a better light. Next comes the fun part. You become a reporter's new BFF. How? By giving them an offer they can't refuse: A package that highlights important details in the suit and provides off-the-record insight. You also provide them fresh angles (as long as it benefits your client, of course).

Some of our clients have benefited from Litigation PR:

- A big entertainment company wanted to use a small firm's trademarked material. So it took it. Didn't ask permission, let alone pay for rights. The small firm fought back, filing suit, and publicizing it worldwide. Shaken by the harsh spotlight, the big company folded its cards and settled.

- An investor sued a well-known wealth manager for mismanaging his money and losing nearly all of it. The financial media loved the story. The wealth manager's well-polished image suffered, and business dried up as his clients shied away.
- Infighting created a schism in a non-profit. Each side was competing to serve the same audience. Backbiting was nasty. Those getting beaten up by the media sought our help. What to do? Steer the media to a storyline that's more favorable to you and undermines your opponents. The other side lost its initial edge and never recovered.

Using litigation for strategic narrative control relates directly to the pattern recognition skills we developed in Chapter 2, where we learned to identify crisis triggers and anticipate how situations will evolve. The same careful assessment that informs when to maintain strategic silence (as we explored in Chapter 3) should guide decisions about when and how to use litigation as a narrative tool.

HANDLING UNCERTAINTY

When you don't have all the facts (and you rarely will), here's your playbook:

The Known-Unknown Framework:

- State what you know (verified facts, NOT speculation)
- Acknowledge what you don't (this is tricky because while transparency builds trust, if you overshare, it'll instill fear and/or anger in people)

- Outline your investigation (depends on the situation, but at least acknowledging an investigation is soon or currently underway shows action)
- Commit to updates (creates accountability)
- Provide resources that your community or audience needs during this period

THE NARRATIVE EVOLUTION

Your crisis narrative needs to evolve through three phases: Immediate Response, Active Management, and Future Positioning.

During the **Immediate Response**, your goal is to acknowledge the situation quickly and clearly. Show that you're aware of what's happening, take responsibility where appropriate, and outline the first steps being taken.

Next comes **Active Management**, where consistency and transparency are key. Show updates as the situation develops, communicate progress, and address concerns head-on. This phase is where leaders can lose or build trust, depending on how they maintain momentum and follow through on initial promises.

Finally, in the **Future Positioning** phase, your messaging should shift from control to growth. Highlight what your company has learned, what changes are being implemented, and how systems are being strengthened. The goal here is to move from defense to resilience.

CONCLUSION

The most powerful crisis response isn't just reactive. It's a carefully constructed narrative that shapes how people understand and remember the events. Throughout this chapter, we've seen how strategic narrative architecture can transform how stakeholders interpret your actions and intentions.

We've explored:

- How controlling the facts allows you to control the story before others define it for you
- The complete spectrum of narrative control, from stopping negative stories to generating positive ones
- How Litigation PR can define the debate on your terms
- The Multi-Platform Protocol that maintains consistency while adapting to different channels
- The three-phase Narrative Evolution that moves you from immediate response to future positioning

Remember the key principle: "If you do the drafting, you get 70% of what you want." When you control the narrative from the beginning, you're shaping how those events will be remembered and understood.

As we transition to Chapter 5, we'll explore how these narrative principles must be calibrated for different digital-first environments, where the speed of information flow and platform-specific dynamics create both new challenges and new opportunities for strategic storytelling. The foundations of narrative architecture remain the same, but the execution requires an entirely new level of sophistication for the digital age.

CASE STUDY:
THE PRODUCT SAFETY NIGHTMARE

Building effective narrative architecture becomes particularly challenging when facing potential product safety issues, where public health concerns, regulatory requirements, and business realities intersect. The following case study illustrates how a food manufacturer used the strategic narrative principles discussed in this chapter to navigate a complex product safety concern. Pay particular attention to how they constructed a narrative centered on transparency and consumer protection, even while facing significant uncertainty about the actual risk level.

Crisis Trigger

A mid-sized food manufacturer discovered that one of their popular snack products might have been contaminated during production. Initial testing was inconclusive but suggested a slight possibility of harmful bacteria in a specific production batch. The company knew of no confirmed illnesses, but the potential risk was significant. Management was split between those advocating for an immediate recall and those concerned about the potential business impact of possibly unnecessary action.

Initial Response

When the company's CEO called me, they were paralyzed by indecision. The company had already spent 48 precious hours debating internally while the potentially contaminated product remained on shelves. I immediately helped them implement our Strategic Response Framework to assess the situation:

- **Impact Assessment**:

  - Potential health risk to consumers (high severity)
  - Consumers, Retailers, Regulators, Employees
  - Financial impact of recall (significant but manageable)
  - Reputation implications (potentially devastating if handled poorly)

- **Stakeholder Mapping**:

  - Consumers (primary concern: safety, fear)
  - Retailers (primary concern: reputation association, imposed upon)
  - Regulators (primary concern: compliance, routine)
  - Employees (primary concern: job security, fear)

- **Response Timeline**:

  - Immediate: Decision on recall
  - 24 hours: Implementation and communication
  - Week 1: Monitoring and adjustment
  - Month 1: Process improvement and prevention

The assessment made clear that despite the uncertainty, the potential harm to both consumers and long-term reputation far outweighed the short-term financial impact of a recall.

Strategic Approach

We developed a comprehensive strategy based on three core principles:

- **Proactive Protection**: Initiate a voluntary recall before any confirmed illnesses or regulatory requirement by demonstrating that consumer safety was the absolute priority
- **Radical Transparency**: Share what was known, what wasn't known, and the decision-making process openly with all stakeholders (Note: not all clients are equipped from a culture perspective for this, so don't force this if your company's known for being very tight-lipped)
- **Operational Excellence**: Execute the recall with precision to demonstrate competence even in crisis

This strategy was implemented through a multi-layered approach:

- **Decision Clarity**: We advised leadership to initiate a voluntary recall of all potentially affected batches
- **Message Architecture**: We focused on a three-layered message:

  - Core facts about the potential contamination and recall
  - Context about the company's safety record and testing protocols
  - Action steps for consumers, retailers, and other stakeholders

- **Channel Strategy**: We created a coordinated rollout across:

  - Direct retailer communications
  - Consumer notices (website, social media, in-store)
  - Media statements
  - Regulatory notifications

- **Leadership Visibility**: We positioned the CEO as the primary spokesperson, demonstrating accountability

Implementation Challenges

Several factors made implementation particularly challenging:

- **Scientific Uncertainty**: The inconclusive testing created an information vacuum
- **Operational Complexity**: Identifying and retrieving specific batches from thousands of retail locations
- **Competitive Opportunism**: Competitors attempted to capitalize on the situation
- **Media Speculation**: Early reporting emphasized worst-case scenarios
- **Social Media Amplification**: Isolated consumer concerns were being amplified across platforms

Resolution Path

The implementation unfolded across four distinct phases:

Phase 1: Decision and Announcement

- CEO made the final recall decision after reviewing the stakeholder analysis
- Recall announcement drafted and approved by legal and communications teams
- Coordinated release to retailers, media, and regulatory agencies
- Website and social media updated with recall information
- Customer service team briefed and prepared scripts were shared

Phase 2: Operational Execution

- Recall logistics implemented with retailer coordination
- Daily progress reports shared with the management team
- Detailed FAQ developed as new questions emerged
- Media updates provided on recall progress, as needed
- Social media monitoring intensified to identify emerging concerns

Phase 3: Testing and Verification

- Additional testing was completed on all production lines

- Third-party verification of safety protocols
- Regular updates provided on testing progress, as needed
- Employee town halls conducted to maintain internal alignment

Phase 4: Process Improvement

- Comprehensive review of production protocols
- New testing procedures implemented
- Updated safety measures communicated to stakeholders
- Long-term monitoring program established

Outcome Analysis

The results demonstrated the value of the proactive approach:

- Testing ultimately confirmed a contamination risk, validating the recall decision
- Media coverage evolved from initial alarm to praise for the company's proactive approach
- Customer surveys showed trust levels actually increased following the recall
- Retailer relationships strengthened through the collaborative recall process
- Sales returned to pre-recall levels within 60 days

What began as a potential reputation disaster ultimately became a case study in effective crisis management.

Lessons Learned

This case illustrates several crucial principles:

- **Lead Don't Follow**: Proactive action before being forced to respond allows control of the narrative
- **Values-Based Decisions**: Prioritizing consumer safety over short-term financial concerns built long-term trust
- **Operational Integration**: Effective crisis communications must be matched by operational excellence
- **Leadership Visibility**: Direct CEO involvement demonstrated organizational accountability
- **Continuous Communication**: Regular updates prevented information vacuums that could be filled with speculation
- **Learning Opportunity**: Using the recall to improve systems transformed a potential disaster into organizational strengthening

CHAPTER 5
DIGITAL-FIRST CRISIS STRATEGIES

EXECUTIVE SUMMARY

This isn't just about social media monitoring or having a good digital presence. It's about fundamentally rethinking crisis management for an environment where digital isn't just another channel, it's the primary battlefield where reputation wars are won and lost.

This chapter focuses on developing crisis strategies for digital environments, where traditional timelines are compressed and platform-specific dynamics dramatically impact effectiveness. You'll learn to navigate the three Digital Crisis Archetypes and implement new leadership roles designed for digital response. You'll learn how to adapt your approach to each environment's unique culture and expectations through platform-specific strategies for TikTok, LinkedIn, Reddit, and other key channels. The chapter provides practical digital tools for monitoring, engagement, content development, and technical infrastructure, creating an integrated approach that combines traditional crisis principles with digital innovation.

When your phone lights up at 3 AM with a notification that your company is trending on X (and not in a good way), you're not experiencing a traditional crisis with a digital component. You're facing a digital turmoil that might have real-world implications.

The rules have changed. Organizations had hours, sometimes days, in the pre-digital era to formulate responses. News cycles were predictable. Information gatekeepers existed. Today, a single tweet can reach millions before your crisis team has even assembled, and a TikTok video can start to define your narrative before you can approve your statement.

THE DIGITAL CRISIS VELOCITY FACTOR

Traditional crisis timelines have been compressed to the point of near imperceptibility. What I call the "Digital Crisis Velocity Factor" has transformed how quickly situations escalate:

Pre-Digital Era

1. Incident occurs
2. Information reaches limited parties
3. Media potentially investigates (hours/days)
4. Story potentially published (days)
5. Public potentially reacts (days/weeks)

Digital Era

1. Incident occurs

2. Information is shared instantly to unlimited audiences
3. Algorithmic amplification occurs (minutes)
4. Public reaction begins (minutes)
5. Traditional media follows digital narrative (hours)

This velocity collapse means organizations must compress what used to be days of decision-making into minutes, often with incomplete information and high emotional stakes.

Consider the airline that experienced a viral video of a tense interaction between a flight attendant and a passenger. In the pre-digital era, such an incident might have remained private or, at worst, become a local news story days later. In today's reality, the video accumulated 2 million views within three hours, sparked a hashtag campaign, and had traditional media calling for comment before the plane had even reached its destination. The airline's standard 24-hour crisis assessment process was utterly inadequate for this timeline.

PLATFORM-SPECIFIC CRISIS DYNAMICS

Each platform has its own personality – X (formerly Twitter) is like the cantina scene from *Star Wars* (anything can happen), LinkedIn is like a *Mad Men* boardroom (professional but still full of drama), and TikTok is like *Wayne's World* (party on, but be authentic about it). Each digital platform has its own distinctive crisis dynamics that require tailored approaches. Understanding these dynamics is crucial for an effective response:

- **Crisis Velocity**: Extremely high, situations escalate in minutes
- **Amplification Mechanism**: Retweets and algorithmic promotion of controversial content
- **User Expectations**: Rapid, direct acknowledgment and transparent updates
- **Response Approach**: Brief, clear statements with regular updates; direct engagement with key influencers; careful monitoring of hashtags

TikTok

- **Crisis Velocity**: Extremely high, can go viral globally in hours
- **Amplification Mechanism**: Creator duets, stitches, and algorithm-driven discovery
- **User Expectations**: Authentic, human response in platform-native format
- **Response Approach**: Authentic spokesperson videos; creator collaboration consideration; avoidance of corporate-speak

Reddit

- **Crisis Velocity**: Medium to high, can build quickly in relevant subreddits
- **Amplification Mechanism**: Upvotes and cross-posting to multiple communities
- **User Expectations**: Detailed information, direct answers to specific questions

- **Response Approach**: AMAs (Ask Me Anything) in appropriate circumstances; community-specific engagement; detailed explanations; avoidance of corporate messaging

Facebook

- **Crisis Velocity**: Medium to high, situations build over hours
- **Amplification Mechanism**: Comments, shares, and group discussions
- **User Expectations**: Detailed explanation and community engagement
- **Response Approach**: More comprehensive statements, active comment management, consideration of paid promotion for crisis updates, private community engagement

Instagram

- **Crisis Velocity**: Medium, visual evidence spreads quickly, but discussion builds more gradually
- **Amplification Mechanism**: Stories, Reels, and visual sharing
- **User Expectations**: Authentic, visually compelling response
- **Response Approach**: Visual statements (carousels, short videos); story updates; influencer relationship management

LinkedIn

- **Crisis Velocity**: Lower than other platforms, but critical for B2B reputation
- **Amplification Mechanism**: Professional sharing and industry commentary
- **User Expectations**: Thoughtful, professional response with business context
- **Response Approach**: Executive statements, industry context; focus on operational and business implications

One luxury retail brand called me in after they learned the hard way after using identical crisis messaging across platforms during a product controversy. Their formal corporate statement worked reasonably well on LinkedIn but was torn apart on TikTok, where users mocked its inauthenticity and created thousands of parody videos. Meanwhile, on Reddit, the statement's lack of specific details led to an investigative thread, where users pieced together a more damaging narrative with incomplete information from the company.

The lesson? Platform-specific approaches aren't optional in digital crisis management. They're essential.

These platform dynamics significantly influence how you'll apply the Strategic Response Framework from Chapter 1 and the Active Silence Protocol from Chapter 3 in digital contexts. The acceleration of crisis timelines in digital environments also impacts how quickly situations move through the crisis stages we mapped in Chapter 2, often compressing what might have been days of development into hours or even minutes.

THE THREE DIGITAL CRISIS ARCHETYPES

Digital crises typically fall into one of three archetypes, each requiring a different strategic approach:

1. The Wildfire Crisis

- **Characteristics**: Explosive growth, broad public interest, high emotional content, rapid spread across platforms
- **Examples**: Viral videos of customer or employee incidents, product failures, executive gaffes
- **Strategic Approach**: Rapid response focused on containment and redirecting the narrative
- **Digital Priority**: Speed, presence across multiple platforms

2. The Slow Burn Crisis

- **Characteristics**: Builds gradually, often in specific communities, and involves technical or complex issues
- **Examples**: Product design controversies, community impact issues, technical vulnerabilities
- **Strategic Approach**: Proactive community engagement and narrative shaping
- **Digital Priority**: Depth over breadth; focused engagement in key communities

3. The Networked Attack

- **Characteristics**: Coordinated actions across platforms, often with an external organization
- **Examples**: Activist campaigns, competitor-driven attacks, politically motivated criticism
- **Strategic Approach**: Network mapping, pattern identification, strategic counter-mobilization
- **Digital Priority**: Intelligence gathering and network disruption

Identifying which archetype you're facing early is crucial for deploying the right digital response strategy.

DIGITAL CRISIS LEADERSHIP: NEW ROLES FOR THE DIGITAL AGE

The digital transformation of crisis management requires new leadership roles and capabilities. They're broken down into role categories, not specifically different people. Often, these are hats one to two people share:

The Digital First Responder

- Authorized to acknowledge issues on social platforms before complete crisis protocols activate
- Trained in preliminary assessment and platform-appropriate holding statements
- Embedded in the digital team with direct crisis team access

The Digital Intelligence Officer

- Responsible for real-time monitoring and pattern recognition (this is often done via a platform that's monitoring and analyzing on your behalf)
- Maps digital influence networks and tracks narrative evolution
- Provides ongoing situational awareness to crisis leadership

The Platform Engagement Specialists

- Platform-specific experts who understand community dynamics
- Capable of authentic engagement in platform-native formats
- Deployed strategically based on where the crisis is gaining traction

The Technical Response Coordinator

- Manages technical aspects of digital response (website updates, SEO considerations)
- Coordinates with IT on potential technical mitigations
- Ensures digital channels can handle crisis-level traffic

A technology company I worked with created a "Digital Crisis Pod" structure where these specialists could be rapidly assembled from various existing team members when needed, rather than maintaining them as a standing crisis team. This approach enabled specialist skills to be deployed precisely when and where needed, without retaining an unsustainable dedicated team.

MICRO CASE STUDY: THE HASHTAG HIJACK RESPONSE

"Environmental activists have hijacked our brand hashtag." A consumer products company discovered that what began as a small campaign by environmental activists against their packaging had been amplified by several influential environmental voices and was gaining mainstream attention within hours.

The Challenge: The company's traditional crisis protocol called for 24 hours of assessment before any response, a timeline that would have allowed the narrative to solidify against them in the accelerated digital environment.

Strategic Response: Rather than following their standard protocol, they activated a digital-first approach: Their "Digital First Responder" acknowledged concerns within 30 minutes; their "Digital Intelligence Officer" mapped key conversation nodes; "Platform Engagement Specialists" crafted platform-specific responses; they launched a new conversation under a different hashtag about their packaging improvement initiatives; and most crucially, they directly engaged the three key influencers driving amplification.

Key Insight: Digital crises require fundamentally different timelines and engagement strategies than traditional crises, with platform-specific approaches and influencer dynamics playing critical roles.

Application: Develop digital-specific crisis protocols that recognize the compressed timelines associated with online reputation threats. Train designated "Digital First Responders" who can identify issues quickly while a complete assessment occurs. Map the digital influence networks relevant to your industry, and build relationships with key voices before crises hit. Most importantly, engage directly within the platforms where conversations are happening rather than trying to pull discussions back to your preferred channels.

THE DIGITAL AFTERSHOCK MANAGEMENT SYSTEM

Unlike traditional crises that typically follow a predictable arc with possible aftershocks (secondary waves of attention that can sometimes exceed the original crisis), digital crises *often* feature aftershocks. These aftershocks usually occur when:

- New information emerges
- Influential commentators discover the story late
- Anniversary dates approach
- Similar incidents occur elsewhere
- Algorithm changes resurface the content

Here are some ways to approach anticipating and managing these digital aftershocks:

- **The Digital Memory Map:** Document exactly what happened, where, when, and with engagement levels to estimate potential resurgence points

- **The Narrative Evolution Tracker:** Monitor how the story changes over time, identifying which elements persist and which fade
- **The Trigger Alert System:** Establish monitoring for specific triggers that might resurface the issue
- **The Rapid Reactivation Protocol:** Maintain the capability to quickly reactivate response resources if aftershocks occur

A gaming company I advised on a specific incident had effectively managed a crisis related to personnel issues, only to face an even larger reputation crisis six months later when a gaming influencer created a retrospective video about the incident that contained numerous inaccuracies. Because they had dismantled their crisis response capability, it took them 72 hours to respond to a video that garnered 12 million views in its first day. The aftershock proved far more damaging than the original crisis.

PRACTICAL DIGITAL CRISIS TOOLS + SYSTEMS

While we can curse digital for getting us here in the first place, we can also thank it for providing tools to manage it. Beyond strategies and structures, specific digital tools can significantly enhance your crisis management capabilities:

Real-Time Monitoring Tools

- **Sentiment analysis platforms** with crisis-specific algorithms
- **Social network mapping tools** that visualize influence relationships

- **Boolean search builders** for precision monitoring across platforms
- **Predictive analytics dashboards** that identify potential escalation

Engagement Platforms

- **Multi-account management tools** for coordinated cross-platform response
- **Community management systems** with crisis-specific workflows
- **Influencer relationship databases** with crisis activation protocols

The key is having these in place *before* a crisis hits because trying to implement new tools and systems is <u>not</u> something you want to be testing during an active crisis.

PLATFORM-SPECIFIC CRISIS STRATEGIES

TikTok has emerged as one of the most challenging platforms for traditional crisis management. Its algorithm can propel content to millions of viewers regardless of follower count, and its creative tools enable rapid remixing that can transform your crisis unexpectedly.

Effective TikTok crisis management requires:

1. Authentic Presence

- Speak the platform's language because corporate messaging fails spectacularly

- Use real people, preferably those already comfortable on the platform
- Embrace imperfection over polished corporate video

2. Creator Engagement

- Identify and engage with relevant creators directly
- Consider a collaborative response with the appropriate creators
- Monitor creator-to-creator influence patterns

3. Format Adaptation

- Use platform-native formats (sounds, effects, styles)
- Create response content that encourages positive engagement
- Consider "stitchable" content that allows constructive dialogue

4. Response Velocity

- Respond within the platform's accelerated timeframe (hours, not days)
- Start with acknowledgment while the complete response is being developed
- Update regularly as the situation evolves

A restaurant chain facing a viral TikTok about alleged food safety issues successfully navigated the situation by having their head chef (not their CEO) create an authentic behind-the-scenes response showing their food safety protocols. The video matched the platform's tone, addressed concerns directly, and invited the original creator to visit their kitchen, thereby turning a potential crisis into content that actually enhanced their reputation for transparency.

Reddit's unique community structure and discussion format require distinctly different approaches from other platforms:

1. Community-Specific Engagement

- Identify which subreddits are discussing the issue
- Understand the specific culture and norms of each relevant community
- Tailor the approach to each subreddit's particular dynamics

2. Transparency Requirements

- Reddit users have extremely low tolerance for corporate messaging
- Provide substantive, detailed information
- Acknowledge limitations and unknowns openly

3. Direct Engagement Format

- Consider AMAs (Ask Me Anything) for appropriate situations
- Respond directly to specific questions and concerns
- Be prepared for challenging and direct questioning

4. Technical Detail Level

- Provide significantly more technical detail than on other platforms

- Anticipate sophisticated analysis and fact-checking
- Have subject matter experts directly engaged

One technology company successfully managed a potential Reddit crisis by having its lead engineer participate directly in discussions about a security vulnerability, providing technical details that would have been inappropriate for general audiences but that satisfied the specific Reddit community's desire for substantive information. They transformed potential critics into advocates by speaking directly to the community in their own language.

CONCLUSION

The most effective digital crisis management is about integrating traditional and digital approaches seamlessly. Digital channels shouldn't be an afterthought in your crisis plan, nor should they replace traditional reputation management principles entirely.

The organizations that navigate digital crises most successfully maintain core crisis management disciplines while adapting them to the unique dynamics of digital platforms. They understand that while the environment has changed dramatically, the fundamental goals remain the same: protecting reputation, maintaining trust, and emerging stronger from challenges.

As we've seen throughout this chapter, this integration requires:

- **Strategic adaptation**: Understanding how traditional crisis principles apply in digital contexts

- **Tactical innovation**: Developing platform-specific approaches that honor each environment
- **Structural evolution**: Creating new roles and systems designed for digital response
- **Cultural transformation**: Building organizations capable of responding at digital speed

The digital landscape will continue evolving, bringing new platforms, challenges, and opportunities. By developing a crisis management approach that adapts to these changes while upholding core reputation management principles, you can effectively navigate the digital challenges that tomorrow brings.

However, even the most sophisticated digital crisis strategy means nothing without strong leadership to execute it. In chapter 6, we'll explore how leaders must show up differently during crises. Because in high-pressure situations, how you lead often matters more than what you say. The digital tools and strategies we've covered provide the foundation, but it's leadership under fire that determines whether your organization emerges stronger or weaker from the crucible of crisis.

CASE STUDY:
THE DIGITAL FIRESTORM

The digital crisis dynamics we've examined throughout this chapter come vividly to life in the following case, where a consumer brand faced a rapidly escalating crisis driven by TikTok. This example illustrates how Digital Crisis Velocity transforms traditional crisis timelines, necessitating fundamentally different monitoring, response, and engagement strategies. Pay particular attention to how platform-specific strategies and real-time adaptation allowed the company to regain narrative control in an environment where minutes (not days) determined success or failure.

Crisis Trigger

A mid-sized consumer brand faced an unexpected digital crisis when a customer posted a video on TikTok showing what appeared to be a foreign object in one of their food products. The 15-second video was captioned with accusations about the company's quality control and manufacturing practices. Within 12 hours, the video had accumulated over 2 million views and spawned hundreds of stitches and duets, many of which added unsubstantiated claims about other quality issues. The hashtag #[BrandName]Fail was trending, and mainstream media had begun reaching out for comment.

Initial Response

When the brand's marketing director called me at 11 PM on a Friday night, they were already in panic mode. Their traditional crisis plan called for a lengthy assessment before any response, but the situation was escalating by the minute. I immediately helped them implement our Digital Crisis Velocity protocol:

1. We conducted an accelerated assessment:

   - Confirmed that the video showed their authentic product
   - Identified the specific manufacturing facility
   - Tracked the spread pattern across platforms
   - Mapped the key amplification nodes driving engagement

2. We established a Digital Command Center with:

   - Real-time social listening across platforms
   - Content production capabilities
   - Technical website support
   - Media monitoring

3. We developed a three-track initial response:

   - Direct engagement with the original poster
   - Platform-specific "holding statements"
   - Background briefing for media inquiries

This accelerated approach enabled us to initiate an active response within a couple of hours, rather than the initially planned 24+ hours for the assessment alone.

Strategic Approach

Traditional crisis approaches would have been dangerously inadequate for this situation. Instead, we developed a digital-first strategy built on three principles:

1. **Speed**: Responding quickly with available information rather than waiting for a complete investigation, which can sometimes take several days to weeks
2. **Platform-Native Engagement**: Meeting the conversation where it was happening in formats appropriate to each platform
3. **Transparent Process**: Sharing the investigation journey in real-time rather than waiting for final conclusions (this was possible due to the detailed tracking the company already utilized)

This strategy was implemented through a multi-faceted approach:

1. **Direct Creator Engagement**: We reached out directly to the original poster, offering to investigate their specific product (free of charge, of course)
2. **Platform-Specific Response**: We created distinct content for each platform:

   - TikTok: An authentic behind-the-scenes video from the QA lab
   - Instagram: Stories showing the production facility's safety measures
   - Facebook: More detailed posts targeting concerned parents

- Website: A dedicated page with comprehensive information
- Note: X/Twitter wasn't utilized because the company didn't have a robust presence on that platform

3. **Influencer Activation**: We engaged relevant industry and platform influencers who could speak credibly to food safety processes
4. **Technical Intervention**: We worked with platform representatives to address demonstrably false copycats that violated platform policies (This is becoming increasingly harder if your company doesn't have a previous working (ahem, financial) relationship with the platform)
5. **Media Strategy**: We provided certain journalists whom we could trust with access to the investigation process, rather than just statements

Implementation Challenges

Several factors complicated our digital crisis response:

1. **Internal Alignment**: Some of the company's leadership struggled with the concept of a transparent, real-time approach, despite having the capabilities to do it
2. **Algorithm Amplification**: Platform algorithms were prioritizing the most inflammatory content
3. **Verification Challenges**: Multiple copycat videos appeared, some with clearly planted foreign objects

4. **Cross-Platform Migration**: The crisis kept jumping between platforms, requiring constant adaptation

Resolution Path

The response unfolded across four distinct phases:

Phase 1: Initial Engagement

- Posted platform-appropriate acknowledgment statements on all channels
- Reached out directly to the original poster (who agreed to send the product for testing)
- Initiated quality control assessment at the identified manufacturing facility
- Provided media with process information rather than defensive statements
- Mobilized quality assurance team for on-camera content (Imagine a less dramatic scene from Monsters, Inc. with the Child Detection Agency, a.k.a. CDA, going after the sock on George Sanderson)

Phase 2: Narrative Reclamation

- Released behind-the-scenes TikTok from the QA lab that quickly gained 1.5M views
- Created Instagram Stories showing real-time investigation updates
- Collaborated with two food safety influencers on explanatory content

- Established a dedicated customer service team for related inquiries

Phase 3: Investigation Transparency

- Live-streamed portions of the testing process
- Released preliminary findings as they became available
- Conducted Reddit AMA (Ask Me Anything) with the head of QC
- Engaged directly with the most prominent users sharing misinformation

Phase 4: Resolution and Learning

- Shared final investigation results (confirming a manufacturing anomaly in a single batch)
- Announced specific quality control improvements (because there's always something more you can do to go above and beyond)
- Implemented enhanced social listening tools
- Conducted a comprehensive review of digital crisis response

Outcome Analysis

The digital-first strategy produced remarkable results:

1. Within 72 hours, sentiment had shifted from 82% negative to 54% positive
2. Several food safety experts publicly validated the company's processes

3. The investigation identified a minor equipment calibration issue that was quickly addressed
4. Sales dipped just 5% during the crisis week before fully recovering
5. The behind-the-scenes content became their most-engaged social media ever (in a positive, not negative kind of engagement)
6. The company's transparent approach was featured as a case study in an MBA program

What could have been a devastating viral catastrophe became a demonstration of the company's values and commitment to quality.

Lessons Learned

This case illustrates several critical principles for digital crisis management:

1. **Platform-Native Engagement**: Each platform requires content that honors its unique culture and format
2. **Transparency as Strategy**: Sharing the process, not just the conclusions, builds credibility
3. **Visual Verification**: In digital crises, showing is significantly more powerful than telling

CHAPTER 6
LEADERSHIP UNDER FIRE

EXECUTIVE SUMMARY

Crisis leadership requires mastering the Three Cs: Calm, Clarity, and Compassion.

How leaders show up during a crisis often matters more than the specific words they say. This chapter develops the essential leadership qualities needed during high-pressure situations and provides practical guidance for working effectively with the media while maintaining control of your narrative. Through the Top 10 Questions framework, you'll prepare for your organization's most critical inquiries during a crisis and learn how to answer them with authority and authenticity.

The COO let out a small laugh during a town hall meeting. That's it. Just a nervous chuckle at the wrong moment during an employee's serious question about layoff concerns. You could feel the temperature drop instantly. By morning, internal messages had leaked, employee forums were on fire, and what could have been a routine corporate restructuring had become a full-blown culture crisis. That single reflexive laugh had just undone months of careful internal communications. That's when I had to deliver some tough love: "In a crisis, leadership isn't optional. It's essential."

THE THREE Cs OF CRISIS LEADERSHIP

In my decades of handling crises, I've found that effective crisis leadership boils down to three core elements: Calm, Clarity, and Compassion. Miss any one of these, and your leadership crumbles.

Calm

A CEO hated cameras. While she was more than happy to be a leader, she was uncomfortable being in the spotlight. Her first challenge wasn't learning *what* to say, it was learning how to maintain composure while saying it. The truth is panic is contagious, but thankfully, so is calm.

Let me share what I taught the camera-shy CEO.

First, we practiced the box breathing technique before every interview. Four seconds in, hold for four, out for four, and hold for four. Repeat. It is simple, and it's remarkably effective at reducing anxiety and maintaining focus. It also seems very LA, but hey, I'm a native Angeleno. I can't help it.

Second, we created mental anchor points: specific phrases or thoughts she could return to when feeling overwhelmed. Similar to the totems in Christopher Nolan's movie *Inception*, where the characters have an object they can privately turn to remind them if they're in a dream.

Third, we used Amy Cuddy's power pose technique as a pre-camera ritual, which included physical grounding exercises: feeling her feet firmly planted, her shoulders relaxed, and her hands steady on her hips like Wonder Woman.

But the *real* breakthrough came when we reframed her perspective. Instead of seeing the camera as a threat (watching your every move and making you feel naked), we trained her to see it as a tool for connection. "Imagine you're speaking to your best friend," I told her. "Someone who wants to understand, who needs your guidance." This mental shift transformed her presence from rigid to relaxed, from defensive to engaging.

Clarity

The most effective leaders understand that confusion feeds chaos, but clarity creates understanding. They practice the art of concise communication, knowing that every unnecessary word dilutes the impact of their message.

They also recognize that different audiences require different approaches. A message that resonates in the boardroom might fall flat in a town hall meeting. Maintaining your core truth while adjusting your delivery to match your audience's needs and expectations is key.

Compassion

When a manufacturing plant closure threatened to devastate a small town's economy, the company's leadership took an unexpected step. They gave 18 months' notice instead of 60 days, established a job retraining program, and worked with local businesses to create new employment opportunities. The CEO attended community meetings, listened to concerns, and adapted the transition plan based on community feedback. This compassionate approach not only helped the community but also protected the company's reputation in other locations.

These three C core leadership qualities are essential for executing the Strategic Response Framework we introduced in Chapter 1 and navigating the crisis stages outlined in Chapter 2. They also connect directly to the empathetic leadership approach we'll explore in greater depth in Chapter 7, where we'll examine how leaders can demonstrate understanding at multiple psychological levels.

THE EXECUTIVE MINDSET: PERSONAL PREP FOR CRITICAL MOMENTS

While organizational readiness is crucial for crisis management, personal mental readiness of key leaders often determines success or failure in critical moments. Based on my work coaching executives through high-stakes situations, here are the essential mindset elements that distinguish effective crisis leaders:

The Psychological Readiness Protocol

Pre-Crisis Identity Anchoring

The most effective leaders during a crisis have clarity about their core values and leadership identity before the crisis hits. This internal anchoring (mostly) prevents reactive decision-making driven by fear or external pressure. I mention "mostly" because there are moments that tempt even the strongest leaders to turn to the Dark Side of the Force. (Yes, yet another Star Wars reference.)

Practice Exercise: Create a written "leadership constitution" articulating your non-negotiable values and leadership principles. Similar to how simply writing down your goals increases the chances of achieving them, writing down your values and leadership principles on paper can also be beneficial. Bonus points for reviewing this document monthly and before major decisions to reinforce your core identity.

Real Example: A healthcare CEO I worked with created a simple three-value anchor: patient welfare first, radical truth-telling, and decisive action. During a potential malpractice crisis, this clarity enabled her to make difficult choices that protected both patients and the organization's long-term integrity.

Emotional Regulation Techniques

Crises trigger the brain's threat response, activating the amygdala and potentially impairing executive function precisely when it's most needed. Effective leaders develop personalized techniques to maintain cognitive control.

Practice Exercise: Develop a personal "emotional reboot" habit: specific actions you'll take when feeling overwhelmed. For some leaders, this involves brief physical movement; for others, structured breathing (like that box breathing exercise I mentioned earlier) or mental reframing exercises.

Real Example: I worked with a CFO who would become visibly flustered during financial crises. We developed a simple three-breath technique paired with a specific grounding phrase. During a significant accounting irregularity crisis, his team noted his remarkable composure using this approach, which preserved both decision quality and stakeholder confidence.

Cognitive Framing Skills

How leaders mentally frame crises dramatically impacts their decision quality. Those who can reframe threats as challenges, obstacles as opportunities, and failures as learning moments demonstrate significantly better performance.

Practice Exercise: Create alternative framing statements for potential crisis scenarios. For example, transform "This is a disaster that could destroy us" to "This is a defining moment where we demonstrate our values and capabilities." But my personal favorite is a meme of a raccoon saying, "There is no trash cannot. There is only trash can!"[6]

Real Example: A retail CEO initially viewed a product safety issue as a legal and financial threat. By reframing it as an opportunity to demonstrate commitment to customer safety, his response shifted from defensive to proactive, ultimately strengthening customer trust beyond pre-crisis levels.

Decision Boundary Setting

Crises often present leaders with impossible choices and information overload. Effective crisis leaders establish clear decision boundaries that preserve focus on what matters most.

Practice Exercise: For your area of responsibility, clearly define: What decisions are yours alone? What decisions should be delegated? What principles will guide your choices when information is incomplete? What time constraints will you operate within?

Real Example: A technology executive I coached established a simple framework for responding to security breaches. Customer data protection decisions were non-negotiable and made immediately; communication timing decisions required consultation but were made within two hours; and brand reputation considerations were addressed only after the technical resolution. This clarity prevented decision paralysis during an actual breach.

Recovery Rituals

Crises deplete mental and emotional resources. Even with your emotional regulation habits, your battery will get depleted. Leaders who establish deliberate recovery practices maintain better decision quality during prolonged, extended crises.

Practice Exercise: Identify your personal recovery needs and establish non-negotiable habits to help fight against running down your sanity battery quickly. These might include sleep minimums, pre-planned meals prepped and ready for you without having to think, or brief calls to your loved ones for an emotional boost.

Real Example: During a months-long corporate restructuring crisis, a COO maintained a 20-minute daily "restoration appointment" blocked off on their calendar involving a specific combo of quiet reflection (which sometimes turned into a micro-nap) and physical movement (burpees or jumping jacks, depending on their mood). This practice enabled sustained high performance that would have been impossible with the constant onslaught that many crises bring.

The Personal Cost of Crisis Leadership

Leading through crisis exacts a personal toll that effective leaders acknowledge and manage proactively. A crisis at work doesn't just impact you and those on the payroll. It also affects your family.

Practice Exercise: Create a personal "early warning system" of indicators that signal you're experiencing excessive strain. For my ultra self-aware executives, you probably already know your tell-tale signs. Just as you can tell when your loved ones are getting hangry, we give off early warning signs when experiencing work-related stress. So, if you're unsure what your little tells are, ask a loved one for honest feedback and enlist them to let you know when you're exhibiting those signs. This also means you have to promise not to snap at them when they do you the favor you asked for.

Real Example: A healthcare CEO I worked with didn't realize how crisis stress was affecting him until his teenage daughter pointed out that he'd started pacing around the kitchen every morning while making coffee, which was something he'd never done before. His wife had noticed he was checking his phone obsessively during family dinners, but his daughter's observation about the pacing was the wake-up call he needed. Together, his family created a simple signal system: when they noticed his stress indicators (such as pacing, phone checking, or his tendency to snap at minor inconveniences), they'd gently say "coffee time": their code for him to take a step back. This early warning system helped him recognize when crisis leadership was bleeding into his personal life, allowing him to implement stress management techniques before reaching a breaking point. The family's involvement not only protected his well-being but also strengthened their relationships during what would otherwise become a sore spot in their memories.

The most effective crisis leaders I've worked with share a common characteristic: they approach personal preparation with the same seriousness and discipline they bring to organizational preparation. Developing these internal capabilities before crises hit creates the foundation for the calm, clarity, and compassion their organizations need during critical moments.

MASTERCLASS MOMENT: RESIST CHOOSING REVENUE OVER PROTECTING YOUR EMPLOYEES

Joy Gendusa, CEO of PostcardMania, an advertising agency, asked her employees on a Zoom call to work in the office during Hurricane Ian, calling the storm a "nothingburger," according to the Washington Post.

Downplaying Hurricane Ian

Let's take a quick look at some of what Gendusa said:

- "Bring your pets, bring your kids, bring everybody to PCM."
- "Obviously you feeling safe and comfortable is of the utmost importance, but I honestly want to continue to deliver and I want to have a good end of quarter."
- "And when it turns into nothing, I don't want it to be like, 'Great, we all stopped producing because of the media and the maybe that it was going to be terrible.'"

The Company Hit The News

When news of the CEO's statements hit social media, Gendusa and the company became instantly famous for all the wrong reasons, and the media frenzy was relentless.

According to the Washington Post[7], several employees felt underappreciated and exploited and feared that if they spoke out publicly, they'd be retaliated against.

The Breakdown Of Bad Optics

The Delivery: The PostcardMania CEO was neither physically present nor had she said she'd be with the employees. Was this a matter of the CEO being willing to risk her team's safety potentially (but not her own) for the sake of profit?

Many companies struggle with employee morale and engagement with a distributed, virtual workforce. But it's especially hard to sell if you ask employees to do as you say, not as you do.

The Mixed Messages: Do you care about safety or profits? Consider this language from the CEO's Zoom message: "Obviously you feeling safe and comfortable is of the utmost importance," followed by: "but I honestly want to continue to deliver and I want to have a good end of quarter."

"And when it turns into nothing, I don't want it to be like, 'Great, we all stopped producing because of the media and the maybe that it was going to be terrible.'"

The tone suggests a clear answer: Revenue is valued most.

The pandemic has taught us to be more compassionate and empathetic towards others. We shouldn't see remarks like this, especially while they were still navigating the COVID-19 pandemic.

The Apology: After receiving social media backlash, the CEO closed Wednesday and Thursday and offered two days of paid time off for those working remotely or volunteering at a shelter.

However, Gendusa's apology rang hollow to the public. It's good that the CEO changed her mind. Still, it felt reminiscent of when another CEO, Tony Hayward of BP, was forced to apologize for complaining publicly that a massive BP oil spill[8] in the U.S. Gulf Coast was an inconvenience for him, and he just wanted his life back.

The Positive PR Attempt: In an attempt to turn the story around, PostcardMania issued a <u>press release</u>[9] showcasing the help it offered to families in need after Hurricane Ian. But then it went on to list its staff's 2022 philanthropic activities, which would make sense during a standard PR blitz. However, issuing this immediately following the negative press draws more attention to the recent coverage and potentially prolongs the issue by creating a related newshook.

This reinforces why the Three Cs of Crisis Leadership (Calm, Clarity, and Compassion) are so crucial. When leaders demonstrate compassion, they signal fundamental values alignment with stakeholder expectations. The absence of compassion in critical moments can cause reputational damage that far exceeds the impact of the initial situation, requiring significantly more extensive recovery efforts.

WHAT DO YOU NEED TO TELL YOUR CRISIS PR PERSON?

EVERYTHING.

The good, the bad, the ugly. If we know the facts, we can craft a believable storyline. As painful as it may be, clients must share their darkest secrets.

If we can hop onto Google and find dirt about you within seconds, so can the media and the opposition. Does something sound fishy or suspect? A private investigator has probably already looked into it and has a manila folder about you stashed away. What will they find?

It's the same for us as it is for lawyers. It's not morbid curiosity. It's critical information. Unless we know it all, we can't create an effective defense, and everybody's reputation is in peril: the lawyer's, the client's, ours.

That's why Crisis PR strategists are brought in under the umbrella of attorney/client privilege. You're hunkered down with senior management. They lay out the problem. Their world seems to be crumbling. Tension is palpable. "Okay…What should we do?" they ask anxiously and fearfully.

Understandably, clients are terrified that the worst will become public. It's fine for them to hope it won't. That's our goal, too. But it's dangerous, actually, to believe it. The most effective way for clients to protect themselves: Hope for the best. Prepare for the worst.

If problems didn't exist, there'd be less need for lawyers, psychiatrists, and other professionals to fix them.

So we start by listening. Not just to the words the client speaks.

Those will only inform you about the superficial. Instead, listen to the tone of his voice and what's being unsaid.

That's the beginning of understanding.

Then, guide the conversation to ferret out what lies beneath the surface. How deep is the dislike between you and...? Do you feel cheated? Tell me more about the history. Did the relationship start out well, then go south? Why? The more you guide and the deeper you drill, the more you learn.

The client may not be purposely withholding information.

He may not realize the relevance. He may not even be fully aware of the undercurrents and how they shape the situation. He doesn't have the benefit of fresh eyes, free of the biases and emotions that color the perceptions of those close to any situation.

Crisis PR is more art than science. It's absorbed by doing: by watching, listening, and feeling until you know in your gut when you've uncovered the essence. Then you can solve the problem.

How eager clients are to share runs the spectrum, but most everyone has an innate tendency to withhold.

Some can't tell you enough. They flood you with more information than you could ever need or use. They talk for hours about matters directly related and incidental. They give you access to their most sensitive files.

The head of a public company recognized that he'd created a mess in the media that could be damaging. He shared everything relevant without hesitation and then kept going for hours in case he'd overlooked anything. Far more than enough information. But it's better to have too much than too little.

Sometimes it's not on purpose. They believe what they're telling you because it comports with their perception of reality. That doesn't make it any better. But perhaps it's forgivable.

Officers of a beverage company eventually shared everything we wanted, but only after being asked the right questions. They weren't trying to withhold. They just presumed that it wouldn't be relevant if we hadn't asked. Full disclosure shouldn't be a guessing game.

Others keep information close and let it out reluctantly in dribs and drabs. They fear that the more you know, the less likely you'll tell their story the way they want it told. One client had the temerity to say, "If you knew the truth, you couldn't defend me with a straight face." They're the most difficult to deal with and the most dangerous.

Some hope that if they hide the truth, it won't be real. And there are a few that straight up know they're lying.

A software company was going to be the target of a "hit piece" in a national magazine. We were assured we'd been told everything. While sitting around a conference table with senior management, an aide delivered the latest inquiry from the reporter. To which the general counsel exclaimed, "He knows about that, too?" Problem was that we didn't know about it, so we were unprepared to defend against it.

Nothing will discredit you faster with the media and the public than being caught in a lie. Once that happens, you've surrendered all credibility. Without credibility, you've lost the battle, if not the war.

It doesn't help to try to excuse it as a half-truth, a fib, or a little indiscretion. Those are just rationalizations. They make it harder to protect the client.

Why the difference? Sometimes, it's basic psychological makeup: the natural extrovert versus the introvert. Those who are most willing to share firmly believe they did nothing wrong and are simply misunderstood. Those who are less willing often fear they may have strayed and are looking for a way out.

Whatever the reason, the lesson is the same: What we don't know can damage everyone.

MASTERCLASS MOMENT: THE EMAIL THAT SAID NOTHING

"We need to say SOMETHING!"

I can practically hear the conversation that led to Target CEO Brian Cornell's all-staff email addressing the company's challenges. Someone in the C-suite felt the pressure of silence during a difficult period and decided that any communication was better than no communication.

They were wrong.

The Challenge: Target faced significant headwinds: eleven straight weeks of declining foot traffic[10], backlash over rolling back DEI initiatives, and tariff impacts hurting their bottom line. Leadership had gone silent during these critical challenges, and employees felt uncertain about the company's direction.

The Strategic Misstep: Cornell's email[11] correctly identified the problem: "silence from us has created uncertainty," but immediately created more uncertainty by failing to provide any substantive solutions or explanations. Instead of addressing *why* leadership had remained silent or *what* they'd been deliberating behind closed doors, the email jumped straight to a vague attempt to reassure.

The Communication Breakdown: The email positioned Target as a passive victim by kicking it off, stating, "There's been a lot coming at us."

Consider what wasn't addressed: declining sales, DEI rollbacks, tariff impacts, or declining consumer confidence. Instead, 40,000 employees received corporate-speak about values being "non-negotiable" and products being "second to none", all while customers shopped elsewhere. It was odd. Management was ignoring the elephant in the room.

Key Insight: This is what happens when the goal becomes "send an email" (or "we just need to issue a statement") instead of solving the underlying problem(s). Communication, for communication's sake, often creates more problems than it solves.

The Better Approach: Effective crisis communication during challenging periods requires:

- **Specificity over vagueness:** Name the actual challenges directly, rather than referring to "headlines and social media." (Sometimes you don't want to repeat the negative(s), but in this case, taking ownership requires being direct, which brings me to my next point.)
- **Ownership over victimhood:** Explain decisions rather than positioning events as things happening "around" the organization.
- **Authentic language:** Skip being defensive when you don't have the receipts to back it up. Saying, "But our values-inclusivity, connection, drive-are not up for debate. They're non-negotiable. Period." is inconsistent with the actions you've just taken.
- **Concrete plans:** Share specific next steps and timelines, not just promises to "communicate more."

It's like a kid saying they're sorry because otherwise they don't get to go out for recess. Make it sound like you mean it and not just paying lip service.

Application: Before sending any crisis communication, ask yourself: Does this actually solve a problem, or does it just make us feel like we're doing something? If your team can't say what specific problem the communication solves, don't send it. The urge to "say something" during difficult times is natural, but ineffective communication often exacerbates situations, rather than improving them.

CAN'T I JUST SAY, "NO COMMENT"?

The media isn't your worst enemy. You may be.

When the media comes calling, it's natural to feel threatened. You shouldn't. You should seize every opportunity and use it to shape the story to your benefit. There's always something you can say or do to make a situation better.

That's why "No comment" is like fingernails on a chalkboard.

If you're in a public brawl or a high-stakes situation where the other side doesn't care about discretion, you'll get beaten up. If you don't tell your story, the other side will tell theirs…and it won't even remotely resemble yours. Then, you'll be left defending against a one-sided story.

People tend to believe the first version they hear. If it's the other side's version, so be it. Your denials will ring hollow and be treated dismissively. When your business and reputation are at stake, the dynamics demand that you communicate early and often.

Your employees, customers, investors, strategic partners, and the public need to be reassured. When there's a threat, they only care about how it affects them and their families. If you fail to inform and reassure, people will fear the worst and speculate about everything that may have gone wrong.

Remember that reporters are just looking for a prominent byline and are generally not out to get you. If you give them something worthwhile for their story, they'll typically leave you alone.

TOP 10 QUESTIONS FRAMEWORK

You'll receive an onslaught of questions from customers, vendors, donors or investors, and the media.

Answering them is the last thing you'll feel like doing. However, if you don't communicate effectively, you risk compromising the organization's reputation.

1. What happened?
2. What does this mean for me? (Varies depending on who's asking. You need to have appropriate responses for each group.)
3. Who's at fault?
4. How did it happen?
5. How long have you known about it?
6. Do you have a history of similar problems?

7. What are you doing to prevent it from happening again?
8. What are you doing to help the "victims"?
9. What are you doing to punish the person(s) at fault?
10. What's next?

Remember: Think about what you want to achieve. Always keep the focus on the message that's most beneficial to you.

WHAT DO I DO IF A REPORTER CALLS?

The short answer: Breathe. Think before you speak. Stick to your talking points. Don't ramble.

The longer answer: Use this decision tree. It's like a high-stakes version of a *Choose Your Own Adventure* book.

Answer the following and see where they lead you.

1. Was this something you planned for?

Yes? Great job! (Jump to No. 2.)

No? Oh, no! It's best to be prepared, but these things happen. (Jump to No. 5.)

2. Do you have a spokesperson?

Yes? Direct reporters to that person. Make sure to follow your media training protocol and don't go off-script. (Jump to No. 3.)

No? You need a designated spokesperson who's been media-trained to deliver a unified message. Select who will be most credible, effective, and reassuring. (Jump to No. 4.)

3. Is your staff trained on whom they should direct the media to?

Yes? You're off to a great start. (Jump to No. 6.)

No? Even if you have a designated spokesperson, it does no good if your staff doesn't know. Without a source of information, the media will grab anyone they can for comment. This means you run the risk of the story going in a direction you don't want. (Jump to No. 9.)

4. Do you have standby statements in place?

Yes? Great, but you aren't done yet. These are only placeholders and must be tweaked or updated as the situation evolves. (Jump to No. 6.)

No? Time is of the essence. Figure out your goal and talking points, fast. (Jump to No. 9.)

5. Can you quickly assemble your crisis team?

Yes? You're ahead of the curve. Everyone must know their roles and work together seamlessly. (Jump to No. 6.)

No? If a member of the team is out of pocket, find their alternate. If you don't have a team at all, you'd better build one, fast. Generally, a crisis team includes the CEO, COO, and CFO; an in-house or outside general counsel; an in-house communications person and outside crisis communications consultant; human resources; the head of IT or an outside IT security consultant; and an insurance agent. (Jump to No. 8.)

6. Do you have all the facts?

Yes? You'll almost never have *all* the facts, especially not in the early stages. Situations are constantly evolving. You must be flexible, and you have to keep people updated as more facts become available. (Jump to No. 10.)

No? Never say or do things based on half-truths or misinformation. Buy yourself some time while you gather facts. The best way to do that is to say, "Let me check on that and get back to you," or "We'll keep you updated as more facts come in." (Jump to No. 7.)

7. Are you considering saying "no comment"?

Yes? Saying "No comment" makes you look guilty. Sometimes, you don't want to (or can't) disclose information. But there's always something you can say or do to make the situation better, or at least less bad. (Jump to No. 8.)

No? Excellent! Tell your story on your terms. (Jump to "How'd you do?")

8. Do you need to buy yourself more time?

Yes? Sometimes, this is necessary while you gather the facts. Don't spread misinformation just because you feel compelled to say something. Stick to your standby statements or talking points. (Jump to No. 4)

No? You need to stay ahead of the story and control the narrative. Grab your standby statements or talking points and keep your stakeholders informed as updates roll in. (Jump to "How'd you do?")

9. Do you have a specific goal you want to achieve?

Yes? Make sure that your talking points support this goal and that you stick to them. (Jump to No. 10.)

No? It's always best to know where you're heading. Select the two to three talking points that best support that goal and stick to them. (Jump to No. 5.)

10. Did the reporter get through to the spokesperson?

Yes? Grab your talking points and remember to breathe. You've got this! (Jump to "How'd you do?")

No? Reporters are usually on a tight deadline. If they left you a voicemail, make sure you get back to them promptly. (Jump to No. 11.)

11. Have more than 15 minutes elapsed since the reporter tried to reach you?

Yes? The window for telling your side of the story is closing fast. It's common for a reporter to have already written the majority of their article by the time they call you for a quick comment to insert before publishing. If you don't respond in time, you risk them reporting that you "could not be reached for comment." You've lost your opportunity to tell your side of the story. (Jump to "How'd you do?")

No? Since reporters are usually on tight deadlines, you still have a chance to tell your side of the story. Grab your talking points and call the reporter back. (Jump to "How'd you do?")

How'd you do?

What you say and do during the first minutes, and certainly the first hour, of a crisis is crucial. It sets the tone for everything that follows. If you lose control during those early stages, you face an uphill battle to get it back. The damage you suffer can be severe.

It's always best to be prepared before a crisis occurs or a reporter calls.

This includes designating a spokesperson and making sure everyone knows where to direct all media inquiries. You must have standby statements ready beforehand, and be flexible enough to update them as the situation evolves.

QUICK TIPS FOR WORKING WITH THE MEDIA

Best thing you can say *(in almost any circumstance)*: "Let me check on that, and I'll get back to you." This gives you time to refine your message. Know what you want to achieve before you start talking.

Worst thing you can say *(in almost every circumstance)*: "No comment." Never miss an opportunity to say something that can shift the spotlight, make the story more favorable, or at least soften the damage.

Pick two or three key points and stick to them. Figure out which ones are most important to you. If you rattle off more than that, chances are the reporter will focus on precisely what you don't want.

Sound bites. They're more likely to get used. Overly detailed statements cause the media (and anyone, really) to lose interest. Be pithy and memorable, but don't forget the substance. Ask yourself: Will this fit neatly into a few seconds of air time or a paragraph in a newspaper? If the answer is "No," go back to the drawing board.

Avoid filling the silence. It's a trap! Most people feel awkward and begin to ramble when reporters fall silent. If you say nothing, they'll realize they've been outmaneuvered and move on.

Media: Friend or foe? Neither. Reporters usually aren't out to get you. Their ultimate goal: Recognition. More often than not, that means a juicy negative story, and you're just in the wrong place at that moment.

Pitching a favorable article. To succeed, you've got to be selling something better than what the reporter currently has, and your storyline must be plausible and substantive. Don't try to put lipstick on a pig.

Conclusion

In moments of crisis, leadership isn't optional, it's essential. As we've explored throughout this chapter, how leaders show up during challenging times often has a greater impact than the specifics of what they say.

We've examined:

- The Three Cs of Crisis Leadership: Calm, Clarity, and Compassion
- The importance of authenticity over scripted responses
- How to work effectively with media while maintaining control

Remember the manufacturing plant closure example? The leadership team didn't just issue a statement; they also took action. They demonstrated genuine compassion through their extended notice, job retraining programs, and community engagement. This wasn't just good PR. Good leadership protected the company's reputation across all its locations.

As we transition to Chapter 7, we'll explore the psychological dimensions of public perception in greater depth. Understanding how stakeholders perceive your actions is the foundation of effective crisis management, and perception rarely aligns perfectly with reality.

CHAPTER 7
NAVIGATING PUBLIC PERCEPTION

EXECUTIVE SUMMARY

Perception, not facts, drives public response to crises.

This chapter explores the psychological dimensions of how stakeholders perceive your actions during a crisis. You'll learn to navigate the Three Levels of Empathy required for effective crisis communication and master the Empathy Action Framework that transforms understanding into impact. The chapter also introduces strategies for battling backlash and shaping perception through selective truth-telling, ethical framing, and authentic engagement that addresses both rational and emotional concerns.

"It's not about the facts," I told the nervous CEO sitting across from me. "It's about what the facts can be made to look like." (A line Eli Gold says on an episode of *The Good Wife*, as well as seasoned Crisis PR managers.) He'd just shown me a 40-page report proving his company had followed every regulation to the letter. Unfortunately, public perception doesn't run on facts; it runs on emotion.

This fundamental disconnect between facts and feelings is at the heart of crisis management. While executives focus on compliance, protocols, and procedures, stakeholders experience fear, anger, and feelings of betrayal. Understanding how people perceive and respond to crises (not how *we* think they should) is the difference between reputation recovery and reputation ruin.

In this chapter, we'll explore the psychological patterns that drive public response, the empathy required to connect with emotional stakeholders, and the strategic approaches needed to shape perception when facts alone aren't enough.

It's not a matter of "If" a crisis will test your understanding of public perception. It's "When." The list of potential reputation threats is daunting: lawsuits, investigations, and employee and executive scandals. Some industries, such as healthcare, food, education, and eldercare, face a higher risk than others. However, all organizations share one vulnerability: the human tendency towards wishful thinking.

We convince ourselves that only the best outcome will happen and believe that the worst won't. We want to conceal problems and control what reaches the public sphere. But as psychologist Amy C. Edmondson notes, "We spontaneously *overvalue* maintaining a sense of comfort, security, and even belonging in the moment, and *undervalue* the vague, probably-won't-even-happen, potentially in the far-off future."[12]

This psychological blind spot creates a dangerous reality: When internal reports surface, warnings emerge, and email trails come to light, organizations appear complicit at best and conspiratorial at worst. In our cynical society, perception becomes reality, and that's all that matters in the court of public opinion.

THE PATTERNS OF PUBLIC RESPONSE

Here's something they don't teach you in business school: Public perception follows predictable patterns. Understanding these patterns is your secret weapon in a crisis. There are three levels of perception. First, **Immediate Perception**. It's what people are saying, how they're reacting, and where they're expressing it. Next is the **Developing Narrative**. Which stories are emerging, who's shaping them, and how they're spreading? Finally, there's **Long-term Impact**. What's likely to stick, which changes are needed, and is it possible to reshape the story?

THE THREE WAVES OF PUBLIC RESPONSE

Public reaction to a crisis doesn't happen all at once. It unfolds in waves, each with its own emotional temperature and strategic risks.

Initial Shock

- Emotional reactions dominate
- Facts matter less than feelings
- Social media amplifies everything

Information Seeking

- People start asking, "Why?"

- Competing narratives emerge
- Stakeholders choose sides

Judgement Formation

- The narrative solidifies
- Long-term perceptions take shape
- Brand loyalty is tested

These waves align with the crisis stages we mapped in Chapter 2, from Initial Shock (similar to Detective Mode) through Information Seeking (paralleling the Critical Window) to Judgement Formation (corresponding to the Shockwave Period). Understanding these patterns enhances your ability to time your responses effectively and construct narratives that resonate at each stage.

THE THREE LEVELS OF EMPATHY

"I don't care how they feel. I care about protecting the company." Those words came from a CEO facing a major product recall. He was correct about the importance of protecting the company: their product met all safety standards, their recall was voluntary, and their legal position was solid. He was also completely missing the point.

Here's the thing about crises, they're never just about what happened. They're about how people feel about what happened. Miss that distinction, and you miss everything that matters.

Here are three critical levels of empathy that every crisis response needs to address:

Immediate Emotional Impact

- What are people feeling right now?
- How is this affecting their daily lives?
- What immediate fears need addressing?

Underlying Concerns

- What deeper worries does this trigger?
- What past experiences color their perception?
- What future implications worry them?

Long-term Relationship Impact

- How does this affect trust?
- What needs to change going forward?
- How can we rebuild stronger connections?

Remember in Ted Lasso when he puts up the "Believe" sign? Everyone thought it was just some corny motivational trick. But Ted understood something fundamental: People don't follow strategies. They follow feelings. The same principle applies in Crisis PR, *except* instead of "Believe," your sign needs to read "We Understand."

MASTERCLASS MOMENT: A SWEET SURPRISE

On a flight from Los Angeles to Denver, a little girl strolled up the aisle with her father in tow. She was passing out little baggies filled with candy to each passenger.

My initial instinct was to be careful. I mean, my father taught me not to take candy from strangers. But then I flipped over the baggie and saw a short note inside:

Hi Fellow Passenger!

My name is Jayde and I am 5 years old and my brother Nathan is 5 months old. We are on our first flight! We apologize in advance if we cry here and there; just know our parents are doing the best they can to keep us cool! (They're more nervous than we are!) We hope you enjoy a few sweets we packed you!

Safe travels!

"Ahhhh, clever girl!" I thought to myself. From a Crisis Prevention perspective, the family deserves a great deal of respect. Had they thought through all the aspects of being proactive and effectively managing a potentially uncomfortable situation? (A baby crying on a plane isn't a "crisis," but the same rules apply.)

A few people jested, "Where are the earplugs?" (How ungrateful. Had no one ever told them it's not nice to look a gift horse in the mouth?)

It's actually wise that the family didn't include earplugs because they have a negative connotation. They're often accompanied by an annoyed grimace and associated with blocking out the bad (construction noise, a significant other who snores, etc.) At the other end of the spectrum is candy.

It brings a sense of joy/happiness and is often accompanied by smiles.

The note was smart.

First, it managed expectations. The parents knew there was a high probability that one (if not both) of their children would let out a yelp of discomfort. So they didn't over-promise by saying they'd keep their kids quiet. They were realistic and showed they were going to make an honest effort.

Second, it told a story. It brought the readers into the lives of this young family and invited us along on their journey. Sharing details about themselves humanized them. Passengers could root for the young parents, who were trying desperately to get their kids through this new experience.

Third, it was thoughtful and unexpected. It's hard to get mad at someone if they've taken the extra effort to show you they understand how their actions might make you feel. (In contrast, how often have you been on a flight and seen the exact opposite?)

What if you don't like candy, or can't eat it? Doesn't matter.

It's the thought that counts. You can always turn around and share it with the person next to you, or with someone else in your life you know will enjoy it.

THE EMPATHY ACTION FRAMEWORK

Empathy without action is just empty words. That's where the Empathy Action Framework comes in: a three-part approach that turns understanding into credibility.

It starts with **Acknowledge**: naming the emotion, validating the experience, and showing you're listening. This is illustrated in the Immediate Response section of the Narrative Evolution, as discussed in Chapter 4. It's the difference between saying, "We're aware of the issue," and saying, "We know people are angry, and they have every right to be."

Next is **Act**: empathy loses value if it's not backed up by movement. Here's where you take visible steps, communicate them clearly, and begin showing tangible progress. Even if the fix is imperfect or ongoing, the action itself sends a message: We're not waiting for the backlash to blow over. We're doing something about it.

Finally, **Adapt** is where leadership maturity is revealed. As new information emerges and feedback rolls in, you update your approach, adjust course, and demonstrate that you're learning and not just reacting. This phase is where your words evolve into proof points, and where short-term empathy becomes long-term trust.

COMMON EMPATHY TRAPS

1. **The Facts Shield** "But we followed all the rules!" Yes, and people still feel hurt. Both can be true.
2. **The Quick Fix** Throwing money at the problem without addressing emotional damage.
3. **The Corporate Robot** Using policy-speak instead of human language.
4. **The Timeline Defense** "We need time to investigate properly." Yes, you do need to investigate, but people are suffering right now and need acknowledgment today, not answers next month.
5. **The Comparison Game** "Other companies have done much worse." While I've never seen anyone flat-out say that in their public response, it's been said in the boardroom. Your stakeholders don't care about other companies, they care about how you treat them.
6. **The Technical Deflection** "Let me explain our complex process..." People experiencing pain don't want a masterclass, they want to feel heard.
7. **The Blame Redirect** "This was caused by external factors beyond our control." Even if true, people need you to own your response, not your circumstances.
8. **The Minimize Move** "It only affected a small percentage of customers." Tell that to the people in that percentage. To them, it's 100% of their experience.
9. **The Legal Shield** "Our attorneys have advised us not to comment." Legal protection that leaves

people feeling abandoned often costs more than legal risk. (I'm *not* advising you to comment on something your legal team has explicitly told you not to. While there are certain instances you can't get into, there's almost always something you can say that's better than "No comment.")

10. **The Process Worship** "We followed our established protocols perfectly." Protocols that allow people to get hurt might point to imperfect protocols that need improvement.

MASTERCLASS MOMENT: THE EMPATHY GAP THAT COST $140 MILLION

The Crisis: In December 2022, Southwest Airlines experienced an operational meltdown that stranded nearly 2 million travelers during the holiday season. While other airlines recovered quickly from a winter storm, Southwest's systems collapsed, resulting in more than 16,900 canceled flights over several days.

The Challenge: Southwest initially focused its communications on technical explanations about weather, scheduling systems, and operational constraints. What passengers desperately needed, however, was an acknowledgment of the emotional and financial toll of missed holidays, stranded families, and travel chaos. The airline's reputation for customer service and operational reliability was built on being "different" from other carriers, which made this failure feel like a more profound betrayal to loyal customers.

The Strategic Misstep: Southwest led with explanations instead of leading with empathy. Its early statements focused on crew scheduling software, network complexity, and operational challenges. While accurate, this was emotionally tone-deaf to passengers sleeping in airports and missing Christmas morning with their families.

The Turning Point: After significant backlash, Southwest eventually shifted its approach. In February 2023, they published a comprehensive message that finally addressed both the technical failures and the human impact, but this empathetic response came *way* too late.

The Long-Term Consequences: The delayed empathy response extended Southwest's recovery timeline far beyond the operational crisis. Swarms of loyal Southwest customers vowed never to fly them again. In December 2023, the Department of Transportation imposed a $140 million settlement[13], 30x larger than previous DOT penalties for consumer protection violations.

Key Insight: During crises with significant human impact, stakeholders need to feel understood emotionally before they're interested in technical explanations. The Three Levels of Empathy (addressing immediate emotional impact, underlying concerns, and long-term relationship implications) *must* precede detailed operational explanations.

The Lesson: Technical expertise without emotional intelligence extends crisis recovery timelines. Southwest's comprehensive February 2023 apology[14], which finally demonstrated an understanding of passenger pain, came too late to prevent regulatory consequences, financial damage, and competitive losses. The path to trust recovery became exponentially steeper because their initial response lacked empathy.

Application: When crafting crisis responses, lead with a genuine acknowledgment of how the situation affects people emotionally. Use specific language that mirrors their experience: not just "we apologize for the inconvenience" but "we understand the frustration of missed family gatherings, stranded children, and holiday plans destroyed." Only after demonstrating this understanding should you transition to explaining what happened and how you'll fix it.

HOW TO ALTER PERCEPTIONS

When devising a strategy to alter perceptions, consider these factors:

- **How's the issue currently framed?** If it's not to your liking, how can you transform it positively?
- **What's the context?** This'll determine how a situation was created and where you can go with it.
- **Is there an existing perception?** If there is, is it good, bad, or neutral?
- **Are you controlling the message?** If so, you have the advantage of being on offense. If not, you're fighting an uphill battle.
- **Are you acting early to pre-empt a problem?** This is the best position to be in. Consider what you can do if you know an unhappy employee is going to sue, an embezzlement will be discovered, an SEC

investigation is coming, or a merger or acquisition is in the works.

- **Is the issue already in the news?** If that is the case, you have less room to maneuver. This doesn't mean you should give up and let the media run wild. But you must analyze your options dispassionately. Which ones are likely to succeed (which may not be the one you'd prefer)?

(For additional thoughts from Eden on how to alter perceptions during a merger, check out her Forbes article "How To Keep Employee Morale High During A Merger"[15].)

BATTLING THE BACKLASH

Public criticism is the acid test of crisis leadership. It's not about becoming immune to backlash and avoiding it altogether, it's about handling it with grace and strategy.

Channel your inner Ted Lasso. When facing the relegation of AFC Richmond, he didn't deny the pain or gloss over the facts. Instead, he acknowledged the reality while maintaining hope and determination. That's crisis leadership 101.

There's an old saying in Crisis Management: "The cover-up is worse than the crime." Let me add to that: "The reaction to the backlash is more important than the initial response."

Let me tell you about a CEO who learned this the hard way. After their initial crisis response sparked intense criticism, they doubled down, defending their position and dismissing the concerns. "We followed all the procedures," they insisted. "People just don't understand." Within 48 hours, what could have been a manageable crisis had turned into an existential threat to the company.

The Five Types of Backlash

Understanding the type of backlash you face is crucial for crafting the right response. Now, there will always be folks who think you've violated one, if not all, of these. They're typically the type of folks who will argue with you about anything you say simply because they don't like you or your company. The goal isn't to win them over; it's to ensure you don't alienate your actual customers.

1. The Authenticity Attack When your response seems off-brand (i.e., scripted, insincere, or corporate)

- Examples: *"Just another hollow corporate apology," "Feels like a PR team wrote this," "They don't mean it"*
- Trigger: Over-polished statements
- Risk: Trust erosion

2. The Adequacy Challenge When your response is viewed as insufficient

- Examples: *"That's all they're going to do?" "That doesn't begin to address the issue," "They clearly just want to check a box and move on"*
- Trigger: Minimal action plans
- Risk: Escalating demands

3. The Accountability Revolt When your response doesn't accept enough responsibility

- Examples: *"They're passing the buck," "They're pretending this was out of their control." "Classic non-apology: We're sorry if you were offended"*
- Trigger: Deflective language
- Risk: Reputation damage

4. The Timeline Tension When your response is perceived as too slow or too late

- Examples: *"Why did it take so long?" "They've had days to say something. This is too little, too late," "They waited to see how bad the backlash got before responding"*
- Trigger: Delayed action
- Risk: Credibility loss

5. The Transparency Test When your response seems to hide information

- Examples: *"What aren't they telling us?" "They're not telling us the whole story," "This feels edited within an inch of its life"*
- Trigger: Information gaps
- Risk: Trust breakdown

COMMON BACKLASH TRAPS

1. **The Defensive Spiral** Defending leads to more criticism, and criticism in turn leads to more defending, which further erodes trust.

2. **The Quick Fix Fallacy** Surface-level solutions and temporary patches mean problems return even bigger.
3. **The Silence Spiral** Avoiding engagement causes an information vacuum, which means others control the narrative.
4. **The Over-Correction** An excessive response makes you look desperate and may also be a waste of resources, which strains credibility.

THE BACKLASH RESPONSE FRAMEWORK

The best place to be is NOT having to battle backlash in the first place. However, if you do find yourself in that position, your response strategy should match the type of backlash you're facing. The specific situation you're in will inform you which options may be best. Don't apply all of them at once.

For Authenticity Attacks:

- **Strip Away Corporate Speak** Replace jargon with plain language, use a more conversational tone, and share personal perspectives.
- **Show Real People** Put faces to the response, share behind-the-scenes efforts, and demonstrate genuine concern.
- **Prove Commitment** Take action, share progress, and demonstrate investment.

For Adequacy Challenges:

- **Strengthen Commitment** Increase the action you're taking by broadening impact, extending timeline, or dedicating more resources.
- **Add Depth** Demonstrate understanding or provide more detail about your planning.

For Accountability Revolts:

- **Own the Issue** Take clear responsibility, acknowledge impact, and show leadership.
- **Demonstrate Understanding** Address specific concerns, show a cause-and-effect grasp, and accept criticism.
- **Lead Change** Drive improvements, set new standards, and show results.

For Timeline Tensions:

- **Explain Process** Share investigation steps, show complexity, and demonstrate thoroughness.
- **Accelerate Action** Speed up response, show progress, and deliver early wins.
- **Maintain Momentum** Regular updates, consistent progress, and clear milestones.

For Transparency Tests:

- **Open the Books** Share more information, explain limitations, and address questions.
- **Create Visibility** Regular reporting, clear metrics, and accessible updates.

- **Enable Verification** Third-party validation, independent review, and stakeholder access.

Remember: Backlash isn't always bad. Sometimes, it's valuable feedback in disgusting packaging. The key is learning to mine for gold in the garbage.

Transform positively by treating criticism as expensive market research you didn't have to pay for. Use that feedback to improve systems that were clearly breaking down. Build resilience by creating processes that prevent similar issues in the future. The organizations that emerge stronger from backlash are the ones that see criticism not as an attack to defend against, but as intelligence about how to do better next time.

Listen actively to what critics are actually saying. Yes, the delivery might be harsh and the tone might be awful, but buried in that anger could be legitimate concerns you missed. Find the truth in criticism, even when it's wrapped in hostility. Identify *valid* concerns that warrant your attention, and delve deeper to understand the underlying causes driving the emotional response. Not every complaint is actionable, but dismissing them all because you don't like the packaging is a costly mistake.

Respond strategically, not emotionally. Address the real issues that surface: the ones that, if you're honest with yourself, you probably knew were problems anyway. Learn to ignore the noise and personal attacks that add nothing constructive to the conversation. Stay focused on what truly matters: fixing legitimate problems and rebuilding trust with people who have valid reasons to be upset.

CONCLUSION

Public perception isn't just about managing the current crisis, it's about building resilience for the future. Every interaction, every statement, every action contributes to your reputation piggy bank. You need to ensure you have enough in there to weather the reputational recessions.

Public perception in crisis management isn't about manipulation but understanding. Your goal isn't to control what people think, but to understand what they feel, address those feelings authentically, and demonstrate through action that their concerns matter. Because in the court of public opinion, perception isn't just reality, it's the only reality that matters.

The psychology of crisis response follows predictable patterns: Initial shock gives way to information seeking, which solidifies into lasting judgement. Your ability to recognize these patterns and respond with appropriate empathy at each stage determines whether your crisis becomes a catalyst for stronger relationships or a permanent scar on your reputation.

When Southwest Airlines focused on technical explanations while passengers needed emotional acknowledgment, they learned that expertise without empathy can extend recovery timelines and deepen trust damage.

As we move into the next chapter, we'll examine how operating in a globally connected world influences your approach.

CHAPTER 8
GLOBAL AND CULTURAL CONSIDERATIONS IN CRISIS MANAGEMENT

EXECUTIVE SUMMARY

What works in New York might get lost in translation in Tokyo. Global crises need local understanding. Adapt your approach to different cultures while maintaining a consistent core message.

This chapter discusses how crisis management strategies must be tailored to different cultural contexts, international businesses, and global crises. Through the Cultural Risk Matrix, you'll learn to anticipate which types of issues might escalate differently across cultural contexts. The chapter examines how fundamental cultural dimensions, including individualism versus collectivism, power distance, uncertainty avoidance, time orientation, and communication style, influence crisis perception and the appropriate response. With the Global Crisis Response Framework, you'll develop approaches that maintain consistency on core elements while allowing for cultural adaptation in implementation.

It's 2 AM in New York when your phone rings. Your Asia-Pacific operations head is calling about a product safety issue that's exploding on social media in Japan. By the time your London team wakes up, it's already trending on X in Germany. Welcome to the reality of global crisis management, where a local incident can become an international reputation threat in hours, and cultural missteps can transform a manageable situation into a full-blown disaster.

I once watched a U.S. food company try to handle a contamination scare in South Korea using its standard crisis playbook. They led with technical jargon and legal distancing, which might have been effective in the United States but fell flat in Korea where food isn't just sustenance; it's an expression of care, family protection, and communal trust. BBQ restaurants, for example, post about which country they source their meat from, believe food is medicine, and love making fresh, seasonal dishes. By skipping over emotional acknowledgment and failing to bow to the cultural gravity many Koreans hold towards food, the company fractured a deeply personal social contract.

Crisis management can no longer operate in cultural isolation in our interconnected world. Let's examine the key dimensions of global crisis management that can significantly impact your international reputation.

The principles we've discussed throughout previous chapters (from strategic silence in Chapter 3 to narrative architecture in Chapter 4 to leadership under fire in Chapter 6) all require cultural calibration when operating internationally. As we'll see in the global cultural misstep case study at the end of this chapter, even domestically, organizations with strong crisis management capabilities can fail spectacularly when they don't adapt their approach to different cultural contexts. The multinational company we'll examine discovered that the same marketing approach that resonated positively in North America created severe reputation damage in Asian markets due to fundamental cultural misalignment.

THE GLOBAL CRISIS AMPLIFICATION EFFECT

When a crisis crosses borders, it doesn't just expand geographically; it transforms. Here's how it works:

- **Language Multipliers**: As your crisis is translated and retranslated across languages, meaning shifts subtly with each iteration, much like the game of Telephone.
- **Cultural Reinterpretation**: Each culture interprets your actions through its own value system, potentially assigning different levels of severity or other motivations to the same behaviors.
- **Regulatory Differences**: What flies in one country may face harsh restrictions in another.
- **Time Zone Acceleration**: The 24-hour news cycle becomes even more compressed when a crisis moves across time zones, giving you less time to respond before the next wave of coverage.
- **Competitive Exploitation**: International competitors may seize the opportunity to gain an advantage in markets where your reputation is newly vulnerable.

THE CULTURAL RISK MATRIX

Not all crisis risks translate equally across cultures. I've developed what I call the Cultural Risk Matrix to help organizations map how different types of issues might escalate differently across cultural contexts:

High Cultural Variability (Approach With Caution)

- **Privacy and Data Issues**: What constitutes privacy varies dramatically across cultures/countries
- **Leadership Behavior**: Expectations for executive conduct differ widely
- **Environmental Practices**: Perceived importance varies by region
- **Workplace Culture**: Acceptable hierarchies and interactions differ greatly
- **Product Marketing**: Images and messaging have varying interpretations

Medium Cultural Variability (Requires Localization)

- **Supply Chain Ethics**: General importance recognized but prioritized differently
- **Corporate Transparency**: Valued broadly but with different expectations
- **Customer Service Standards**: Universal importance but varying expectations
- **Community Relations**: Valued across cultures but with different emphasis
- **Diversity Practices**: Growing global importance but varying definitions

Low Cultural Variability (More Universal Standards)

- **Product Safety**: Consistently high importance across cultures
- **Financial Integrity**: Broadly similar expectations globally
- **Corruption**: Generally viewed negatively (though tolerance varies)
- **Worker Safety**: Consistent baseline expectations
- **Child Protection**: Universal high importance

This matrix helps organizations anticipate where they might need culturally specific crisis approaches versus where more standardized responses might work effectively.

This risk assessment approach complements the Crisis Assessment Matrix we introduced in Chapter 2, adding the critical dimension of cultural variation. When combined with the Stakeholder Mapping techniques from Chapter 2 and the Strategic Silence Decision Tree from Chapter 3, this matrix helps organizations determine which issues require culturally specific approaches versus where more standardized responses might be appropriate.

NAVIGATING CULTURAL VALUES IN CRISIS RESPONSE

Each culture has deeply held values that shape how crises are perceived and what constitutes an appropriate response. Here are critical dimensions to consider:

Individualism vs. Collectivism

- **High Individualism Cultures** (U.S., Australia, UK): Emphasize personal responsibility, prefer direct acknowledgment of who's responsible, expect individual leaders to take visible action
- **High Collectivism Cultures** (Japan, China, many Latin American countries): Focus on group harmony, may prefer organizational responses over individual ones, place a high value on protecting relationships
- **Crisis Application**: A CEO who steps down immediately after a crisis might be viewed as appropriately accountable in an individualistic culture but as abandoning responsibility in a collectivist one.

Power Distance

- **High Power Distance Cultures** (Many Asian and Middle Eastern countries): Expect leadership to maintain authority during crises, may view excessive apology as weakness
- **Low Power Distance Cultures** (Scandinavian countries, New Zealand): Expect flatter hierarchies and collaborative crisis response, value leadership vulnerability
- **Crisis Application**: A town-hall approach to crisis communication might work well in Denmark, but could undermine leadership credibility in Malaysia.

Uncertainty Avoidance

- **High Uncertainty Avoidance Cultures** (Germany, Japan, South Korea): Prefer detailed plans, thorough explanations, and transparent processes during crises
- **Low Uncertainty Avoidance Cultures** (UK, India, Singapore): More comfortable with ambiguity, they may accept broader reassurances without detailed plans (Note: India's lower uncertainty avoidance reflects a tolerance for ambiguity in principle, though in practice, many organizations still expect detailed plans and hierarchical approvals, especially in high-stakes situations. Singapore is often classified as low in uncertainty avoidance due to its globalized outlook, though its strong regulatory culture can demand clear crisis protocols.)
- **Crisis Application**: A German audience might find a "we're looking into it" response inadequate, while a British audience might accept the same statement if delivered with appropriate confidence.

Long-Term vs. Short-Term Orientation

- **Long-Term Oriented Cultures** (China, Japan, Germany): Focus on sustainable solutions and long-term reputation impact
- **Short-Term Oriented Cultures** (U.S., many Latin American countries): Prioritize immediate impact mitigation and quick resolution

- **Crisis Application**: A crisis response focusing on immediate compensation might resonate in Brazil but seem short-sighted in South Korea, where articulating long-term preventive measures might be more valued.

Communication Styles: High vs. Low Context

- **High-Context Cultures** (Japan, China, Arab countries): Rely heavily on implicit communication, contextual understanding, and reading between the lines (Note: There's a variation between Gulf countries and Levantine cultures. There's also a difference in state-driven communication norms and interpersonal trust dynamics.)
- **Low-Context Cultures** (U.S., Germany, Scandinavian countries): Value explicit, direct communication with clear statements
- **Crisis Application**: A straightforward American-style crisis statement may seem appropriately transparent in Germany, but it could be perceived as bluntly inappropriate in Japan, where more nuanced messaging is expected.

THE GLOBAL CRISIS RESPONSE FRAMEWORK

Building on these cultural dimensions, here's my framework for developing globally effective crisis responses:

- **Core and Culture Separation** Distinguish between your non-negotiable core response (facts, actions, remedies) and culturally adaptive elements (communication style, spokespeople, emphasis).

- **Cultural Response Mapping** For each primary market, map the cultural dimensions that will most impact crisis perception.
- **Local Validation** Never assume cultural understanding. Always validate your approach with trusted local experts before implementation.
- **Regional Response Coordination** Ensure regional teams can act with appropriate autonomy while maintaining global consistency on core elements.

BUILDING A GLOBAL CRISIS RESPONSE STRUCTURE

The most effective global crisis management starts with having the right team structure in place before any crisis hits, but even with perfect cultural understanding, implementing an effective global crisis response remains challenging. Here's a comprehensive approach that addresses both structure and implementation:

The Three-Tier Team Architecture

Global Crisis Core Team

- Sets consistent global strategy, core messaging, and non-negotiable standards
- Monitors cross-market developments and identifies potential regional escalation
- Coordinates resources and knowledge sharing between regions

Regional Crisis Units

- Adapt global strategy to regional cultural contexts
- Maintain relationships with local stakeholders and media
- Implement culturally appropriate response tactics

Cultural Advisory Network

- Provides cultural interpretation and guidance during crisis development
- Validates proposed approaches before implementation
- Identifies potential cultural vulnerabilities in global strategy

This structure balances the need for consistency with the reality that effective crisis management must be culturally relevant to work.

Making It Work: Four Implementation Systems

1. The Tiered Approval System Develop clear guidelines that delineate:

- What messaging requires global approval
- What can be adapted regionally with notification
- What can be fully determined at the local level

2. The Cultural Translation Process Move beyond literal translation to cultural translation by:

- Working with local teams to identify cultural nuances
- Testing messages with local focus groups, if possible
- Incorporating cultural adaptation into standard crisis protocols

3. The Global-Local Liaison Role Designate specific individuals responsible for:

- Translating global strategy into culturally appropriate implementation
- Feeding local insights back to the global team
- Maintaining consistency while enabling appropriate adaptation

4. The Cultural Simulation Program Prepare through regular crisis simulations that:

- Involve teams across multiple cultural contexts
- Test scenarios with specific cultural complications
- Develop muscle memory for cross-cultural coordination

This integrated approach ensures you have both the right people in place and the systems to coordinate them effectively across cultural boundaries.

THE DIGITAL DIMENSION OF GLOBAL CRISES

The digital landscape adds another layer of complexity to global crisis management, creating both challenges and opportunities:

Digital Challenges in Global Crisis Management

- **Platform Fragmentation**: Different platforms dominate in different markets (WeChat in China, LINE in Japan, Kakao Talk in Korea, WhatsApp in India and Brazil)
- **Regulatory Variation**: Digital communication rules vary dramatically (GDPR in Europe, Great Firewall in China)
- **Information Flow Control**: Ability to manage message spread varies by platform and region
- **Translation Issues**: Automatic translation tools can create dangerous misinterpretations (PLEASE be cautious with these!)

Digital Opportunities in Global Crisis Management

- **Direct Communication**: Ability to speak directly to stakeholders without media filtering
- **Real-Time Monitoring**: Capability to track reaction variations across markets simultaneously
- **Cultural Calibration**: Options to tailor messaging for different audiences
- **Response Agility**: Capacity to adjust quickly as cultural reactions become clear

Effective global crisis management leverages these digital opportunities while mitigating the risks.

CONCLUSION

In today's interconnected world, organizations that master cross-cultural crisis management build a significant competitive advantage. The ability to maintain trust across diverse cultural contexts becomes a strategic asset that extends far beyond crises.

As one global CEO told me after successfully navigating a complex international crisis: "We thought we were just protecting our reputation. What we didn't expect was how much stronger our relationships would become in markets where our competitors stumbled over cultural blind spots."

Utilize cultural adaptation as a strategic opportunity to demonstrate respect, foster deeper connections, and establish the kind of trust that transcends borders and sustains reputations even during the most challenging times.

As we'll explore in Chapter 9, building this kind of crisis-resistant culture requires more than just cultural awareness; it demands a fundamental commitment to the values and practices that build resilience across all dimensions of your organization.

CASE STUDY:
THE GLOBAL CULTURAL MISSTEP

The cultural dimensions and global crisis dynamics we've explored in this chapter aren't abstract concepts. They're critical factors that determine how your crisis management will be received across different markets. The following case study illustrates how a multinational corporation learned this lesson the hard way, and how culturally calibrated responses ultimately transformed a reputation disaster into an opportunity for cultural learning. Note how different cultural contexts required fundamentally different approaches to apology, remedy, and relationship repair.

Crisis Trigger

A multinational corporation headquartered in the United States faced a serious reputation crisis when a marketing campaign that had been successful in North America was launched in several Asian markets with minimal adaptation. The television commercial that used humor around family dynamics was perceived as disrespectful to elders in several key Asian countries. The backlash began on social media in South Korea, quickly spread to China and Japan, and soon escalated to calls for boycotts, government criticism, and international media attention.

Initial Response

I was brought in 48 hours after the crisis began, when the company's initial statement explaining the humorous intent of the advertisement had only intensified the backlash. The situation had already escalated to:

- Trending hashtags calling for boycotts across multiple Asian countries
- Officials publicly criticizing the company
- Major retailers in China removing products from prominent display
- Western media beginning to cover the "cultural insensitivity" story
- Internal tension between regional offices and headquarters

We immediately initiated our Global Cultural Assessment protocol:

- We assembled a crisis team that deliberately included senior leaders from the affected regions
- We conducted a rigorous cultural analysis of the advertisement with local experts
- We mapped stakeholder expectations across different cultural contexts
- We analyzed the specific values being violated in each market
- We identified the distinct apology expectations in each cultural context

This assessment revealed fundamental misalignments between the campaign's humor and deep-seated cultural values regarding family hierarchy and respect for elders. More critically, it showed that the company's initial explanation was being perceived as doubling down rather than acknowledging the cultural offense.

Strategic Approach

It was clear that a standardized global response would fail. Instead, we developed a culturally calibrated strategy based on three principles:

- **Cultural Humility**: Demonstrating genuine understanding of and respect for cultural differences
- **Local Leadership**: Empowering regional leaders to lead the response in culturally appropriate ways
- **Meaningful Adaptation**: Going beyond words to show commitment through concrete actions

This strategy was implemented through a comprehensive approach:

- **Campaign Withdrawal**: Immediate removal of the offensive advertisement from all markets
- **Local Empowerment**: Regional leaders are given authority to implement market-specific remediation
- **Structural Reform**: Overhaul of the company's global marketing approval process

Implementation Challenges

Several factors made this situation particularly complex:

- **Internal Cultural Divisions**: Tension between headquarters and regional offices over decision authority
- **Media Cross-Contamination**: Coverage in one region affects perceptions in others

- **Social Media Amplification**: The crisis jumping platforms and borders in unpredictable patterns

Resolution Path

The implementation unfolded across four phases:

Phase 1: Immediate Correction

- Withdrew the campaign from all markets globally
- CEO issued an initial acknowledgment of the concerns
- Empowered regional leaders to lead local responses
- Paused all global marketing temporarily
- Established 24/7 monitoring across all regional markets

Phase 2: Culturally Calibrated Response

- Regional leaders conducted market-specific engagements
- Released distinct statements tailored to each cultural context

Phase 3: Demonstrative Action

- Implemented a new marketing review process with local cultural consultation
- Conducted a comprehensive review of all global marketing materials
- Created a cross-cultural training program for marketing teams

- Established regional advisory councils for future campaigns

Phase 4: Sustainable Reform

- Restructured the global marketing organization to increase regional input
- Implemented cultural sensitivity training across the organization
- Created a global-local balance framework for future campaigns

Outcome Analysis

The culturally calibrated approach led to differentiated outcomes across markets:

- Overall Business Impact: Sales declined 18% in Asian markets during the crisis but fully recovered within one quarter
- Long-term Outcome: The company's new culturally-informed marketing process became a competitive advantage

What began as a significant global reputation crisis ultimately led to a transformation in the company's approach to cross-cultural marketing.

Lessons Learned

This case illustrates several essential principles for global crisis management:

- **Cultural Calibration**: Different cultures require fundamentally different crisis responses
- **Power of Humility**: Genuine cultural humility resonates across markets
- **Local Empowerment**: Regional leaders must have the authority to lead culturally authentic responses
- **Beyond Translation**: Effective global crisis management goes far beyond linguistic translation to cultural translation
- **Structural Solutions**: Sustainable resolution requires organizational changes, not just communication changes

CHAPTER 9
BUILDING CRISIS-RESISTANT
CULTURES

EXECUTIVE SUMMARY

The best crisis defense is built on ordinary Tuesdays. Strong company culture prevents more crises than any emergency response plan ever will.

Most organizations invest heavily in crisis response capabilities while ignoring the cultural foundations that determine whether crises occur in the first place. This chapter explores how to build crisis-resistant cultures through the Five Pillars: Transparency, Accountability, Proactivity, Resilience, and Trust. You'll learn to recognize the warning signs of cultural drift that make organizations vulnerable, measure your culture's health through four key diagnostic areas, and navigate the stages of cultural evolution from awareness to continuous improvement. Most importantly, you'll discover how to make crisis preparedness feel like organizational excellence rather than overhead, creating cultures where problems get solved before they become headlines.

"I can't believe this is happening. We never saw it coming."

The most surprising part of this sentiment is how often the warning signs were usually there, flashing like neon billboards in Las Vegas.

A manufacturing company's safety inspector noticed a pattern of minor equipment failures but hesitated to report it because the last person who raised safety concerns was labeled a "troublemaker" and passed over for promotion. Three months later, that equipment failed catastrophically, injuring two workers and triggering an investigation that led to the company paying $50 million to fix. The crisis wasn't caused by the equipment failure, it was caused by a culture that punished truth-telling.

THE FIVE PILLARS OF CRISIS-RESISTANT CULTURE

You probably didn't make it out of business school without hearing someone say, "Culture eats strategy for breakfast." It's often attributed to management guru Peter Drucker, but MIT professor Edgar Schein[16] is actually who we should be thanking. In crisis management, I'd add that culture can either be your strongest shield or your most significant vulnerability. The difference frequently comes down to whether people feel safe speaking up when they see problems brewing.

Typically, failure in one or a few of these pillars leads to a crisis. If these pillars are solid, your chances of facing a full-blown crisis are drastically reduced.

Pillar 1 - Transparency: The Early Warning System

Transparency isn't just about having an open-door policy; it's about creating an environment where bad news travels as fast as good news. When employees feel safe bringing problems forward without fear of being blamed for them, minor issues get fixed before they become front-page-worthy scandals.

I once worked with a tech company where the CEO started every all-hands meeting by sharing one thing that wasn't going well. These were not catastrophic failures but real challenges (missed deadlines, customer complaints, competitive pressures, etc.). The message was clear: problems aren't signs of failure; they're opportunities for improvement. When a security vulnerability was discovered six months later, three engineers independently reported it within a few hours of one another. Compare that to organizations where employees stay silent until problems explode.

What transparency looks like in practice:

- Leaders who publicly acknowledge their own mistakes and course corrections
- Regular "failure parties" where teams share what went wrong and what they learned
- Skip-level meetings where senior leaders hear directly from frontline employees
- Anonymous reporting systems that get investigated, where employees see results (unlike a suggestion box to nowhere)

Pillar 2 - Accountability: Owning the Outcome

Real accountability is about ownership. When something goes wrong, crisis-resistant cultures ask, "How do we fix this?" before they ask, "Who's responsible?" They ask both questions and ensure the answers lead to *meaningful* change.

A healthcare client of mine faced a medication error that could've been devastating. Instead of covering it up or scapegoating the nurse involved, the leadership team conducted a thorough investigation, found systemic issues in their medication management process, redesigned the entire system, and shared their learnings with other hospitals. The nurse who made the initial error became part of the solution team. Now, that's accountability in action.

What accountability looks like in practice:

- Clear ownership of outcomes, not just tasks
- Leaders who model accountability by taking responsibility for team failures
- "How did our systems allow this to happen?" instead of "Who screwed up?"
- Learning from mistakes instead of hiding them

Pillar 3 - Proactivity: Seeing Around Corners

Crisis-resistant organizations don't waste their resources responding to problems; they anticipate and prepare for them. They build early warning systems, conduct regular risk assessments, and create contingency plans for scenarios that might never happen. Although the latter is kind of a chicken or the egg quandary: Did the incident not occur because they had systems in place beforehand to nip the issue in the bud, or did the issue just never occur naturally? The challenge is that crisis preparedness feels expensive when you don't need it and invaluable when you do.

One of my financial services clients conducts quarterly "pre-mortems" where teams imagine that a major initiative has failed and work backward to identify what could go wrong. It sounds morbid, but it's incredibly effective. They've prevented three potential crises in the past two years simply by asking, "What if this goes sideways?"

What proactivity looks like in practice:

- "What could go wrong?" becomes a standard question, not a pessimistic afterthought
- Regular scenario planning exercises
- Investment in prevention, not just response
- Trend monitoring and pattern recognition

Pillar 4 - Resilience: Bouncing Back Stronger

Resilience is about having the adaptability and resources to handle situations when they arise. Resilient organizations build redundancy into their systems (always having a backup for key functions), cross-train their personnel (always having folks on the bench who can step in with little to no additional training), and maintain reserves (financial, emotional, and operational) for tough times.

During the pandemic, I watched two similar retail companies handle the crisis very differently. Company A had built resilience into its operations: diversified revenue streams, cross-trained employees, strong cash reserves, and a culture of "figuring it out together." Company B was leaner and more efficient in good times, but had absolutely no buffer for disruption. Guess which one not only survived but thrived?

What resilience looks like in practice:

- Redundancy in critical systems and processes
- Cross-functional training so people can step into different roles
- Financial and operational reserves for unexpected challenges
- A culture that views setbacks as temporary and solvable

Pillar 5 - Trust: The Foundation of Everything

Trust is the currency of crisis management. Make sure you're making deposits in good times, so that you can make withdrawals when things take a downturn. When stakeholders trust your organization, they give you the benefit of the doubt during difficult times. When they don't, every mistake becomes evidence of deeper problems.

Trust is built in small moments over long periods. It's the supplier who gets paid on time every month, the customer service rep who goes the extra mile to solve a problem, and the CEO who admits uncertainty instead of pretending to have all the answers. When a crisis hits, that accumulated trust (a.k.a. your reputation) becomes your most valuable asset.

What trust looks like in practice:

- Consistent follow-through on commitments, especially small ones
- Putting stakeholder interests ahead of short-term profits
- Admitting when you don't know something instead of making it up
- Transparent communication about both successes and challenges

Remember in *Jurassic Park* when Dr. Malcolm warns that "life finds a way"? Well, in my world, crises find a way. You can have all the protocols and policies in the world, but without the right culture, a crisis will always find a crack to slip through.

THE WARNING SIGNS

Your culture is constantly sending you signals about its health. The key is learning to read them before they become crisis symptoms. Think of a crisis-resistant culture like your immune system. You can't prevent every threat, but you can build natural defenses that make your organization more resilient.

Red Flags: Cultural Warning Signs

Fear of speaking up is perhaps the most dangerous red flag. When employees stop bringing forward concerns, you lose your early warning system. Problems fester in silence until they explode publicly.

Pattern denial is when organizations refuse to acknowledge recurring issues. "That was a one-time thing" becomes the standard response, even when the same problems keep happening.

Reactive decision-making means you're always playing catch-up. Decisions get made in crisis mode, without proper analysis or stakeholder input. This creates a chaotic environment where small problems quickly become big ones.

Information hoarding occurs when knowledge becomes power, and people protect their turf by controlling the flow of information. You'll see this in organizations where different departments operate in silos and don't communicate with each other, where meetings occur behind closed doors, and where asking questions is perceived as a challenge to authority.

Blame-shifting creates a culture where nobody wants to be associated with problems. When something goes wrong, the first instinct is to point fingers rather than solve the issue(s), leading to a vicious cycle where problems worsen because nobody wants to own them.

Green Flags: Signs of Cultural Health

Open dialogue means people feel safe disagreeing, asking questions, and raising concerns. Meetings include diverse perspectives, and leaders actively seek out dissenting opinions.

Pattern recognition means the organization learns from experience and adjusts accordingly. When similar issues arise, people notice and take action before they become crises.

Proactive planning includes regular risk assessment, scenario planning, and "what if" discussions. Prevention gets as much attention as response.

Problem-solving focus means the organization treats challenges as puzzles to solve rather than disasters to survive. There's a genuine curiosity about root causes and systemic solutions.

Shared responsibility creates collective ownership of outcomes. When something goes wrong, teams ask, "How do we fix this together?" instead of "Who's to blame?"

THE WARNING SIGNS IN ACTION

Let me tell you about two companies I worked with that faced similar issues with product quality.

Company A (Walking Red Flag): When quality problems surfaced, the production manager blamed the suppliers, the suppliers blamed the specifications, and the engineering team blamed the production processes. Nobody wanted to own the problem. Each department closely guarded information about defect rates (and sometimes fudged).

When a customer complained, it took weeks to trace the issue because nobody had a complete picture. By the time leadership got involved, the problems had escalated to the point where a major recall was inevitable.

Company B (Smooth Sailing): When similar quality issues arose, the initial response was a cross-functional team meeting involving production, engineering, suppliers, and customer service. Data was shared openly. The conversation focused on "How did our system allow this to happen?" and "What do we need to change?" They discovered the issue was a miscommunication between engineering and production about specification tolerances. The fix was implemented within a week, preventing any customer impact.

Same problem, different cultures, completely different outcomes.

MASTERCLASS MOMENT: THE $3 BILLION CULTURE LESSON

The Crisis: In 2016, Wells Fargo was caught creating millions of unauthorized customer accounts, driven by an aggressive sales culture and unrealistic quotas that incentivized employees to commit fraud. What started as a scandal about fake accounts quickly turned into something much more profound.

The Challenge: Wells Fargo initially attempted to manage the situation with carefully worded statements and limited accountability, framing it as the actions of a few bad apples rather than systemic failure. The bank's leadership failed to recognize that this wasn't fundamentally a comms problem but a values and culture problem that no PR statement could fix.

The Strategic Misstep: Instead of immediately addressing the cultural rot that created the conditions for widespread fraud, Wells Fargo tried to manage their way out with traditional crisis response tactics: controlled messaging, scapegoating lower-level employees, and minimal leadership accountability.

The Turning Point: Eventually, Wells Fargo realized that real recovery required a complete cultural overhaul, including eliminating sales goals, restructuring the board, implementing new governance systems, and demonstrating sustained behavioral change rather than just promising improvement.

The Long-Term Consequences: Wells Fargo's cultural crisis became a case study of how deep-rooted organizational failures create consequences that extend far beyond any news cycle:

- **Financial Impact:** Over $3 billion in fines and settlements by 2020[17]
- **Regulatory Punishment:** The Federal Reserve imposed unprecedented growth restrictions from 2018 through June 2025[18]
- **Leadership Exodus:** Multiple CEOs struggled to repair the damage: John Stumpf resigned in 2016, Tim Sloan stepped down in 2019, and Charles Scharf took over with a mandate to transform the entire culture

- **Reputation Collapse:** By 2022, Wells Fargo still ranked lowest among major banks in customer reputation metrics[19], despite years of image repair efforts

Key Insight: When a crisis stems from fundamental organizational failures, communications alone can't solve the problem. Real cultural and operational change must precede any effective reputation recovery.

The Lesson: Crisis prevention through cultural integrity is exponentially more effective than even the most sophisticated crisis response. (Caveat: But having great cultural integrity doesn't give you carte blanche to have a ham-handed reaction.) Organizations that invest in building values-aligned cultures may avoid these decade-long recovery journeys entirely. As Wells Fargo discovered, rebuilding stakeholder trust requires more than addressing past failures; it demands consistently demonstrating new values through actions *over time*.

Application: When facing a potential crisis, ask yourself: Is this a communication problem or a values problem? If your organization's actions don't align with its stated values, fix the actions first. No statement, however well-crafted, can bridge that gap. The journey back to trust is measured in years, not news cycles, and requires demonstrable change rather than just promises of improvement.

(For additional thoughts from Eden, check out the LA Times Story "Wells Fargo Must Do More Than Fire Its CEO to Mend Its Image, Critics Say"[20].)

MEASURING CULTURAL HEALTH

"But Eden," clients often ask, "how do we know if our culture is really crisis-resistant?"

Here's your diagnostic framework. Think of it as taking your organization's vital signs.

Response Speed: How Fast Does Truth Travel?

In healthy cultures, problems surface quickly. Bad news doesn't get filtered or delayed as it moves up the organization. You can measure this by tracking how long frontline issues take to reach decision-makers.

Key questions: How quickly are issues reported up the chain? How long does it take to mobilize resources when problems arise? Do frontline employees feel comfortable escalating concerns?

What good looks like: A manufacturing plant where machine operators have direct communication channels to plant management, and safety issues get addressed within hours, not days.

What bad looks like: A financial services firm where compliance issues sit in middle management for weeks while they "investigate further" before informing senior leaders.

Information Flow: How Freely Does Knowledge Move?

Information flow reveals a great deal about an organization's culture. In crisis-resistant organizations, information moves horizontally (between departments) as easily as it moves vertically (up and down the hierarchy).

Key questions: How freely does information move across departments? How accurate is the intelligence reaching decision-makers? How transparent is communication about challenges and failures?

What good looks like: A tech company where engineers, sales, and customer success teams have weekly cross-functional meetings to share insights about product performance and customer feedback. (Not to be mistaken for having a meeting for meeting's sake. Make sure valuable conversations are being had.)

What bad looks like: A retail organization where the marketing team launches a promotion without consulting operations, leading to inventory shortages and customer dissatisfaction.

Team Cohesion: How Strong Are the Bonds?

Team cohesion isn't about everyone being friends (or, worse, family); it's about shared purpose and mutual support during challenges. Strong teams pull together during crises instead of fragmenting under pressure.

Key questions: How strong is trust between different departments? How aligned are actions across the organization? How well do teams collaborate during pressure situations

What good looks like: A hospital where doctors, nurses, and administrators work seamlessly together during emergencies, with clear roles and shared accountability for patient outcomes.

What bad looks like: A consulting firm where different practice areas compete for resources and clients, leading to duplicated efforts and confused messaging.

Learning Capacity: How Well Do You Evolve?

Organizations with high learning capacity treat every challenge as a source of intelligence. They systematically capture lessons and apply them to prevent future problems.

Key questions: How does the organization handle mistakes and failures? What systems exist to capture and share lessons learned? How quickly does the organization adapt based on experience?

What good looks like: An airline that conducts thorough post-incident reviews for every safety event, shares findings across the entire fleet, and updates procedures based on learnings.

What bad looks like: A software company that experiences the same types of security vulnerabilities repeatedly because they don't have processes for learning from previous incidents

THE FOUR STAGES OF CULTURAL EVOLUTION

Building a crisis-resistant culture isn't a one-time initiative. It's an ongoing process that requires sustained attention and investment.

Stage 1: Opening Your Eyes Most organizations underestimate their cultural vulnerabilities.

Conduct cultural assessments through surveys, focus groups, and behavioral observation. Look at near-misses and small problems as indicators of larger cultural issues. Acknowledge that your current culture might not be sufficient for future challenges.

Stage 2: Getting Everyone on Board Cultural change requires leadership commitment and employee engagement.

You need to have leadership teams that model the behaviors they want to see, clearly communicate about why cultural change is necessary and how it benefits everyone, and involve employees in designing solutions rather than imposing changes from above.

Stage 3: Making It Real Change happens through consistent action over time.

Regularly practice new behaviors, even when inconvenient. (Just having a gym membership doesn't make you fit. You have to put in the work.) Measure systems that track cultural indicators, not just business metrics. Celebrate examples of the new culture in action.

(Who doesn't love to be celebrated?!? Positive reinforcement!)

Stage 4: Continuous Improvement Culture isn't static (at least not *healthy* ones). It requires ongoing attention and adjustment based on experience and changing conditions.

Conduct regular cultural health check-ups. Be willing to adjust your approaches based on what works and what doesn't. Recognize that cultural evolution is an ongoing process, not a destination to be reached.

MAINTAINING CRISIS RESILIENCE

"We fixed everything after the last crisis," my client said proudly. "New policies, new procedures, and new people." Then he paused. "So why do I feel like we're more vulnerable than ever?"

Remember that scene in *Groundhog Day* where Bill Murray keeps waking up to the same day? That's what happens when organizations don't maintain their crisis resilience. They face a crisis, fix it, get comfortable...then wake up to basically the same crisis in a different form. The key is building maintenance into your organizational rhythm, not treating it as optional when times are good.

THE DRIFT PHENOMENON

Ever notice how boats drift off course without constant course corrections? Organizations do the same thing. I call it "crisis drift": the gradual, often imperceptible movement away from crisis-ready practices.

Crisis drift occurs due to human nature. When things are going well, crisis preparation feels like unnecessary overhead. Training sessions get shortened. Drills get skipped. Policies don't get updated. Standards slowly erode through thousands of small compromises.

The Five Warning Signs of Crisis Drift:

Shortened or skipped crisis drills "What's the harm in skipping over some steps or the session just this once? I mean, why did we schedule this in the middle of our busy season?" This thinking treats crisis preparation as optional when business is good, exactly when you can most afford to invest in it.

Delayed policy updates "We'll get to it eventually. What are the chances something will hit in the meantime?" Policies become outdated, procedures don't reflect current reality, and gaps develop in your defense systems.

Reduced team training "We're already facing death-by-meetings. Do we need to have everyone take the time to do this?" Crisis skills are like muscles; without regular trips to the gym, you'll lose your gains

Informal protocol modifications "It's scribbled down somewhere in one of our meeting notes. We'll remember to get it later." Famous last words. Small workarounds become standard practice, but they're not documented or communicated, creating confusion during actual crises.

Complacent attitudes "Meh. We haven't seen a full-blown crisis in years. Do we really think it's going to happen?"

Success breeds overconfidence, and overconfidence breeds vulnerability.

I worked with a food processing company that had implemented excellent safety protocols after a contamination incident in 2018. By 2021, their safety record was spotless, and the incident felt like ancient history (and not because COVID warped our memory of time). Gradually, shortcuts crept in. Safety meetings became monthly instead of weekly. Equipment inspections got delayed when production schedules were tight. New employees received abbreviated training because "they'll learn on the job."

In 2022, they had another contamination incident. It wasn't because their systems were inadequate, but because their culture had drifted away from the discipline that made those systems effective in the first place. The second crisis was entirely preventable, but preventing it would have required vigilance during the three years when nothing was going wrong.

THE LEADERSHIP CHALLENGE

"But Eden, we can't keep crisis prevention at the top of everyone's mind forever."

Actually, you can. But it doesn't require constant paranoia. It requires building crisis-resistant thinking into your organizational DNA.

The secret is making crisis preparedness feel like excellence, not an added cost. When you frame it as "how world-class organizations operate" rather than "disaster planning," people embrace it as a competitive advantage rather than a necessary evil. (Is that spin? No. It's changing your perspective.)

Five Ways to Operate Like a World-Class Organization:

- **Celebrate preventive actions:** Publicly acknowledge teams and individuals who identify and address problems before they become crises. Create awards for "Best Catch" or "Best Prevention."
- **Share near-miss learnings:** Regularly communicate stories about problems that were prevented or caught early. This reinforces the importance of vigilance and demonstrates that preventive efforts are valued and encouraged.
- **Reward early warning reporting:** Make it career-enhancing, not career-limiting, to bring forward concerns. People must see that truth-telling is valued and rewarded, not frowned upon or punished.
- **Make it part of performance reviews:** Include crisis-prevention behaviors in performance evaluations. Recognize people who surface problems early, suggest improvements, or prevent potential issues. (*Caveat:* Don't put a minimum reporting requirement in place because you'll end up with faulty data. Folks will feel compelled to bring anything they can possibly skew to hit their reporting requirement.)
- **Build it into promotion criteria:** Include crisis-leadership capabilities in advancement decisions.

Signal that crisis preparedness is a core competency for organizational success.

CONCLUSION

Building a crisis-resistant culture isn't about creating a culture of fear. It's about building organizational excellence that naturally includes crisis resilience as a core capability.

Organizations that master this don't just survive crises; they use them as catalysts for becoming stronger, more trusted, and more resilient. They understand that culture is both their strongest defense and their most valuable competitive advantage.

Remember: The best crisis defense is built on ordinary Tuesdays, in the small decisions and daily interactions that either strengthen or weaken your organizational immune system. Invest in culture with the same rigor you apply to strategy, operations, and finance. When a crisis strikes, culture determines whether you emerge stronger or weaker on the other side.

CHAPTER 10
AI, THE FINAL FRONTIER?

EXECUTIVE SUMMARY

AI's better at impersonating the CEO than the CEO's actual assistant.

This chapter explores the double-edged nature of artificial intelligence in crisis communication: how it threatens to unravel trust, and how it can become your strategic advantage when wielded wisely. You'll learn to lead through a world where deepfakes, voice clones, and generative avatars blur the line between truth and trickery. Just as critically, you'll develop tools to avoid panic, set guardrails, and build a culture that's resilient even when everything looks fake.

THE ERA OF UNREAL REALITY

Gone are the days when seeing is believing. We're living in a *Black Mirror* episode where seeing is no longer believing, and the only way to tell reality from simulation is to build relationships so authentic that fakes feel obviously wrong. Welcome to the brave new world of deepfakes and AI-generated content.

Remember when a professionally photoshopped image was the height of digital manipulation?

Those days seem quaint compared to what we're facing now. Today's AI can create videos so convincing that even family members might be fooled into paying scammers. It can clone voices from just a few minutes of audio samples. It can generate seemingly authentic emails, social media posts, and even news articles that appear to come from legitimate sources.

This isn't science fiction -- it's Monday morning's potential crisis.

Even seasoned professionals are getting tricked. Just ask the COO who almost hired the "perfect candidate." The candidate showed up on Zoom with enviable credentials, charisma, and pitch-perfect answers. They were almost ready to send an offer letter heading into the second round interview, when the COO had a weird gut feeling. She asked the candidate to wave his hand in front of his face. He refused. Turns out, he was an AI-generated avatar the entire time. The COO, a tech-loving geek, was almost fooled.

If even tech-loving experts are struggling to discern what's real, what hope do the rest of us have?

THE VERIFICATION PARADOX

The Verification Paradox is the idea that just when the need for verification has never been greater, the tools we rely on to verify are breaking down.

In 2024, an employee paid out $25 million after having a video conference call with someone they thought was their CFO[21]. And it turns out that it wasn't just the CFO who was fake, it was everyone else on the call, too. The scammers had created an elaborate deepfake to lull the employee into thinking he was safe. We've just surpassed the "uncanny valley" where the small tells we could sense from a video that signaled to us that this is fake have vanished.

This is the verification paradox: the more sophisticated the fakes become, the harder they are to disprove, and the more damage they can inflict before the truth (if it can be established at all) catches up. It's a race between fiction and reality, and your reputation is in the crosshairs.

THREE LEVELS OF AI CRISIS THREATS

Think of AI crisis threats like a video game with increasingly difficult levels. Each level requires different strategies, and ignoring any level can be catastrophic.

Level 1: Externally Generated Fakes (The Obvious Threat)

This is what everyone's worried about: deepfake videos of your CEO saying terrible things, voice clones authorizing wire transfers, or fake social media posts that go viral. It's like someone wearing a really good mask of your face and robbing banks.

Common scenarios:

- Deepfake videos of executives making inflammatory statements
- Voice clones used to authorize financial transactions
- Fake social media posts appearing to come from official accounts
- Manipulated audio from earnings calls or interviews

The kicker: These are actually the easiest to defend against because they're external attacks that you can prepare for.

Level 2: Internal AI Misuse (The Insider Threat)

This is where your own people become the problem -- employees misusing AI tools, AI systems making biased decisions, or well-meaning staff accidentally creating compliance nightmares.

Real example: A marketing manager at a mid-sized company used AI to generate customer testimonials for their website. Seemed harmless until folks on Instagram noticed that some of the "customers" had the same writing style and started digging. Trust was eroded not just with potential customers, but also with current ones, who wondered if they had been sold lies.

Other scenarios:

- HR using biased AI for hiring decisions
- Automated customer service replies without human review

- Employees using AI to write reports without verifying facts or leaking confidential information
- Poorly written AI prompts that make discriminatory decisions in lending, insurance, or services

WHEN AI IS SMARTER THAN YOUR CULTURE

Context Meets Consequence

Meet Hertz's AI damage scanners. In theory, they sound like a great idea, like an "MRI for rental cars" that flags a car's bumps and bruises. In reality? They've become the poster child for tech sprinting ahead of judgement.

In Atlanta, a renter was hit with a $350 fee[22] for an alleged scuff flagged by the system. Like a Magic Eye Image that some claim to see only after being told what it is, this was a spot so tiny that you had to zoom in 5X to even notice it. It was something a staff member would have never dinged the customer for.

To make matters worse, their attempt to resolve the dispute got routed through an automated chatbot that led nowhere. There was no human in the loop. Hertz's claims of "fairness and transparency" ring hollow when human review is a near-impossible maze. The irony? The person renting the car advises companies on how to implement AI and automation.

Why It Matters for Crisis PR

This isn't just relegated to the rental car industry. Rolling out AI without aligning it with customer expectations or without anticipating edge-case scenarios is a PR crisis waiting to happen.

Here are some things to consider when doing your AI roll-out plan, from a damage-control perspective:

- Is there a human override?
- Do you have clear communication with users *before* an AI-generated action affects them?
- Is there a way to capture and honor cases where "tech flags" are technically correct but contextually unfair?

AI's exciting, and it's changing *constantly*. Before embarking on implementing it, work with an expert who's up to date on what's happening. For a more exhaustive list of things to consider before implementing AI, check out this AI Readiness Checklist[23].

Level 3: Authenticity Erosion (The Existential Threat)

This is the scariest level because it's not about any specific fake -- it's about people losing trust in *everything*. When stakeholders begin to question whether any content is genuine, traditional crisis communication breaks down entirely.

The problem: Even when you're telling the truth, people might not believe you because they don't know what's real anymore. It's like being the *Boy Who Cried Wolf*, except everyone else was crying wolf too, and now nobody believes anyone. "Is this real?" becomes the default.

THE GROK FIASCO: AI GONE ROGUE

In July 2025, xAI, the Elon Musk–led company behind Grok, found itself in the crosshairs after the bot began posting controversial content, got banned in Turkey for criticizing its president, (very likely?) contributed to the sudden departure of X CEO Linda Yaccarino, and forced the company to take the bot offline[24]. Among Grok's worst offenses: antisemitic slurs, Holocaust denial, and support for Hitler that culminated in it referring to itself as "MechaHitler."

The company's apology cited a rogue code path and an overly compliant language model, but critics pushed back arguing that Grok initiated some of its worst content without prompting. For executives, this is a cautionary tale about delegating voice without oversight. AI can be a force multiplier for good, but it can also supercharge the damage.

ETHICAL AND LEGAL ACCOUNTABILITY

Where does liability lie when AI causes damage? If your AI tool posts something defamatory, makes a discriminatory decision, or spreads false information, is the company on the hook? Is it the developer? Is it the person who signed off on the specific feature causing the issue? The courts and regulators are still sorting this out, but here's what you should assume for now: the buck stops with you.

- **Ownership of AI mistakes** If the words go out under your name or your company's brand, they're yours. Full stop. AI needs checks and balances. A human (or group of folks) need to do a final round of approval before AI-generated content is shared publicly.

- **Defamation and Discrimination** Just because "the bot did it" doesn't mean you avoid lawsuits or regulatory heat. (Looking at you, Grok.)
- **Apologies and AI** A human apologizing for an AI's actions still needs to take responsibility. Passing the blame to "the algorithm" makes you look like you've lost control of your own operation.

Bottom line: If you're using AI, you're accountable for it.

THE NEW RULES OF STRATEGIC TRUST

1. **Trust Before Crisis** Build trust capital now so your audience knows what you sound like when you're not in crisis.
2. **Lock Down Your Channels** Use consistent platforms, voices, and formats so people spot a fake faster.
3. **Have a Verification Hub** Designate a single, fast-to-update space (URL, social channel, intranet) where people can verify info.
4. **Train Like It's Real** Run simulations that include deepfakes and AI misinformation. Your team shouldn't be surprised when it happens.

BUILDING AI-RESISTANT CULTURAL PRACTICES

How do you protect your organization against threats that can materialize in minutes, look completely authentic, and spread globally before you've even finished your morning coffee? The answer lies not in reactive measures, but in building AI-resistant cultural practices and strong cybersecurity. Since things are moving so quickly in this space, scammers may have already found a workaround for these by the time you're reading this, so consult with someone in real-time about the latest best practices:

Establish Authentication Protocols

- Create verification systems for major announcements (like multi-factor authentication, but for communications)
- Develop private confirmation codes or phrases known only to key executives
- Implement digital signatures and blockchain verification for critical content
- Train employees to verify unusual requests (payments, personnel, or policy changes, etc.) through secondary channels

Strengthen Trust Reserves

- Build stronger, more authentic relationships with stakeholders before crises hit
- Regularly communicate through established, verified channels
- Educate your audience about how you officially communicate
- Create a track record of transparency that makes fakes less credible (Warning: The double-edged sword is that the more data available, the easier it is for scammers to use it in building their deepfakes.)

WHEN & HOW TO USE AI WISELY

It's not all bad. When used wisely, AI can be a crisis superpower tool.

Crisis Monitoring at Scale

Media monitoring isn't new, but some still aren't familiar with the magic. AI can scan millions of posts, articles, and videos, in real time, flagging potential issues before they have a chance to explode. It can detect sudden shifts in sentiment, identify clusters of emerging narratives, and track keywords tied to your executives, products, or brand. Done right, this gives you an early-warning system that alerts you when the conversation is starting to tilt, so you can respond before a spark turns into a firestorm.

Predictive Modeling

AI can analyze a vast amount of data to predict how your stakeholders might react to a crisis. By using machine learning, AI can forecast how a situation might affect your brand's reputation and provide data-driven insights. This can help you make informed decisions.

Bias Disruption

One of AI's underappreciated strengths is its ability to surface blind spots that leaders might be too insulated to see. It may flag tone-deaf language before it goes live, highlight unintentional slants in messaging, and help anticipate how different stakeholder groups might interpret your statements. Used wisely, it can add a layer of perspective that makes your communication harder to weaponize against you.

Crisis Simulation

One of the best ways to prepare for a crisis is to simulate one. AI can help you create a list of possible crisis scenarios so you can practice your response. It can help you identify gaps in your Crisis PR plan, improve your messaging, and build your team's confidence.

Drafting Support

Reduce communication packet turnaround time. When a crisis hits, every second counts. It's essential to communicate with your stakeholders quickly and efficiently. With AI, you can draft statements and responses that can be reviewed and enhanced by your Crisis Team (legal, marketing and communications, crisis PR professionals, etc.) This can help you craft messaging consistent with your brand's voice and values. Think of it as Mario (as in Super Mario Bros.) using his power-ups to navigate through the different challenges while staying true to his mission.

AVOIDING AI PITFALLS

Confidential information: Beware of inputting confidential, proprietary, or privileged information that could harm your company if it becomes public. Just as you would exercise discretion and carefully consider what you put into an email or text, consider the potential consequences of sharing your company's sensitive information online.

Limited scope: AI generates insights based on the data it has been trained on, which means you will need a more comprehensive approach, especially if you've purposefully avoided inputting privileged or confidential information. Entrepreneurs should be mindful of this limitation and supplement AI's insights with other sources of information and expertise to ensure they have a well-rounded view of their decisions.

Lack of personalization: While AI can help craft messaging quickly, it's essential to remember that Crisis PR requires a personal touch. Stakeholders want to know that you care about their concerns and take their feedback seriously. That's why it's crucial to balance the speed of AI with the personalization that comes from working with a (human) PR professional. The outcome will be better messaging with minimal wasted effort.

Overreliance on technology: While AI can provide data-driven insights, it's only part of the puzzle. When navigating a crisis, human judgement, intuition, and experience are indispensable. You need to consider all aspects of your Crisis PR plan to ensure your brand's reputation stays strong and, with luck, your crisis appears invisible (at least temporarily).

BEST-IN-CLASS AI GUARDRAILS

Think of these as your "hit the brakes" signals. If your AI starts doing any of the following, stop it immediately, investigate, and take it offline if needed:

- Generating anything that could be seen as hateful, discriminatory, or personally damaging
- Publishing "factual" claims that haven't been verified by a trusted human source
- Impersonating someone (inside or outside your company) without clear, documented consent
- Sharing confidential or sensitive internal data
- Responding to prompts in ways that contradict your brand values or compliance rules

Before anything AI-generated leaves your four walls, run it through a human sniff test:

1. Would I be comfortable reading this on the front page of *The New York Times* tomorrow?
2. If challenged, can we prove the "facts" are accurate?
3. Does it sound like something *we* would actually say?
4. Could someone misinterpret this as offensive, biased, or misleading?

If any of those make you hesitate, don't hit "publish."

THE AUTHENTICITY IMPERATIVE

If there's one lesson to take from the rise of AI-generated content, it's this: authentic human connection has never been more valuable. Organizations that cultivate genuine relationships, communicate transparently, and build cultures of trust will be naturally more resistant to synthetic disruption. Your stakeholders are more likely to doubt content that doesn't align with their direct experiences with you, employees will flag weird behavior sooner, and executives can resist knee-jerk panic when a fake emerges.

In an age where anything can be faked, being consistently real becomes your most significant competitive advantage.

CONCLUSION

The digital landscape will continue to evolve, bringing new platforms, new challenges, and new opportunities. However, you can navigate whatever digital challenges tomorrow brings by developing a crisis management approach that adapts to these changes while maintaining core principles of reputation management.

You don't need to be a technologist. But you do need to be a leader who understands how trust, narrative, and authenticity evolve in an AI-driven world. Always remember: In this game, sometimes you need a power-up, but you still have to be the one holding the controller.

In the final chapter, we'll zoom out from the tools and threats to focus on the mindset that turns crisis managers into strategic masters.

CHAPTER 11
THE STRATEGIC MIND

EXECUTIVE SUMMARY

The difference between crisis management and crisis mastery isn't in the frameworks. It's in the strategic thinking that sees three moves ahead.

After decades of managing crises that range from "mildly annoying" to "company-ending," I've learned that what separates good crisis managers from truly strategic ones isn't what they do, it's how they think. The frameworks and tools we've explored throughout this book are just the beginning.

Think of it like the difference between knowing all the moves in chess and being able to think like Magnus Carlsen. Or the difference between following a recipe and being Gordon Ramsay (ideally, minus the yelling).

"Eden, we have a problem." I've heard those words so many times that I can often autocomplete their sentence just by the way they say my name. But over the years, I've noticed something interesting about the calls I get. The executives who reach out aren't usually facing their first crisis. They're often seasoned leaders who've handled difficult situations before. So why are they calling me?

Because they've hit the limits of conventional crisis management thinking. They've realized that crisis management isn't really about managing crises at all, it's about understanding the *strategic* forces that create them, shape them, and ultimately determine whether they become disasters or opportunities.

Welcome to the strategic mind. It's like the moment in *The Matrix* when Neo stops seeing the code and starts seeing the patterns underneath. Except instead of dodging bullets in slow motion, you're dodging reputation disasters before they happen. So, are you taking the blue or red pill?

Follow me.

THE $50 MILLION PATTERN

A manufacturing company learned the hard way what happens when you manage events instead of understanding systems.

The Surface Problem: Equipment failure led to worker injuries and a massive recall.

The Strategic Reality: Three months earlier, a member of the Quality Assurance team noticed a pattern of minor equipment failures but hesitated to report it. Why? Because the last person who raised safety concerns was labeled as a "troublemaker" and passed over for promotion.

The $50 Million Question: Was this really an equipment crisis, or a culture crisis that happened to manifest through equipment?

Here's where strategic thinking diverges from crisis management. A crisis manager would have focused on the immediate response: medical care for workers, recall logistics, media statement(s), regulatory compliance, etc. All necessary, all important.

A strategic thinker would have asked different questions:

- What created the conditions where safety concerns couldn't surface?
- How many other "troublemakers" are staying silent right now?
- What other systems might fail because early warning signs are being suppressed?
- How do we transform this liability into a competitive advantage?

The company opted for a crisis management path. They handled the immediate situation professionally, paid the $50 million, and moved on. Three years later, they faced an identical crisis with a different piece of equipment. Same pattern, same cultural root cause, same expensive outcome.

That's the difference between managing events and understanding systems.

THE THREE LEVELS OF STRATEGIC THINKING

Throughout this book, we've built your crisis management toolkit. Like a chess grandmaster who can see the endgame developing while amateur players are still figuring out their next move. Or like Enola Holmes (Sherlock's little sister), who spots the real clue while everyone else is distracted by the obvious red herrings. A strategic mind is constantly reading signals and adjusting its strategy as needed.

Most people see crises as random events that strike without warning. Weather happens. Equipment fails. Employees make mistakes. Competitors attack. Activists organize. The media pounces.

But that's surface-level thinking. It's like watching a disaster movie and thinking the real problem is the volcano/asteroid/alien invasion, when the actual problem is that nobody listened to the scientist who saw it coming in Act One.

After managing hundreds of crises, you begin to see the invisible architecture emerge from the subtle patterns and underlying forces that determine not just whether a crisis will occur, but also how severe it will be, how it will unfold, and whether an organization will emerge stronger or weaker. After being part of thousands, you can just sense it instinctively.

Now, let's talk about how strategic minds use these tools differently.

Level 1: Framework Application

This is what everyone does and where most people stop. They learn the Strategic Response Framework from Chapter 1, apply it when crises hit, and execute well. This is good crisis management.

Level 2: Pattern Recognition

Strategic thinkers begin to see patterns across seemingly disparate situations. They recognize that the hidden letter in Chapter 2 and the product recall in Chapter 4 had early warning signs. They use the Crisis Assessment Matrix not just during crises, but to prevent them.

Level 3: System Design This is mastery. Strategic minds use crisis experiences to redesign the conditions that create crises. They don't just implement the Five Pillars of Crisis-Resistant Culture from Chapter 9; they use each crisis to strengthen all five pillars simultaneously. They do this by asking: How does this crisis change the game itself? What new vulnerabilities has it created? What new capabilities has it revealed? How can we use this experience to build antifragility against entire categories of future threats?

STRATEGIC THINKING IN ACTION: THE DECISION TREE

Here's how to develop your strategic mind using the framework you already know:

When Any Issue Surfaces, Ask:

Immediate Questions (Crisis Management Level):

- What happened? (Chapter 2: Crisis Anatomy)
- How do we respond? (Chapter 3: Strategic Silence)
- What's our narrative? (Chapter 4: Narrative Architecture)

Strategic Questions (Pattern Recognition Level)

- Why did this happen now? (Chapter 9: Cultural Warning Signs)
- What similar patterns exist elsewhere? (Chapter 2: Early Warning System)
- How does this connect to our stakeholder relationships? (Chapter 7: Public Perception)

System Questions (Strategic Design Level)

- What systemic changes does this reveal that we need to implement? (Chapter 9: Five Pillars)
- How can we use this to build a competitive advantage? (Chapter 8: Global Considerations)
- What capabilities do we need to prevent entire categories of similar issues from arising? (Chapter 10: AI, The Final Frontier?)

THE STRATEGIC PARADOXES

Here's where crisis management gets really interesting: conventional wisdom is often wrong.

Paradox #1: The Best Crisis Managers Rarely Manage Crises

The most strategically sophisticated executives I work with aren't crisis response experts, they're crisis prevention artists. They've learned to see problems when they're still opportunities and address vulnerabilities *before* they become big problems.

But here's the twist: they didn't develop this capability by studying crisis prevention. They developed it by understanding the strategic forces that create crises in the first place. They're the ones who call me weeks to months before a decision needs to be made, asking for advice about how an issue may play out if they take various approaches. They like options and value their peace of mind.

Paradox #2: The Safest Organizations Are Often the Most Vulnerable

I've watched "low-risk" organizations get destroyed by minor incidents while "high-risk" companies navigate major disasters with barely a scratch. The difference? Organizations that acknowledge risk as part of the game build antifragility. Organizations that believe they're safe build brittleness.

Paradox #3: The Best Crisis Response Is Usually Invisible

The most successful crisis management often looks like nothing happened at all. No dramatic statements, no heroic leadership moments, no inspiring comeback stories. Just strategic moves that defuse situations before they become situations.

That invisibility is exactly what makes it a strategic advantage. It's why folks are shocked when someone asks for an example of a crisis that was handled well, and my response is, "The ones you never see." It's why some of our greatest successes are the ones you never get to hear or read about.

BUILDING YOUR STRATEGIC MIND: THE PRACTICE

Strategic thinking isn't innate. It's developed through deliberate practice. Here's how to build these capabilities:

The Weekly Strategic Review Every week, ask yourself: What patterns am I seeing across different issues? How are the frameworks from this book connecting in real situations? What early warning signs might I be missing?

The Monthly System Audit Once a month, evaluate: Which of the Five Pillars needs strengthening? How is our Cultural Health (Chapter 9) trending? What new vulnerabilities are emerging?

The Quarterly Strategic Simulation Every quarter, run scenarios: What would happen if our most significant cultural weakness became a crisis? How would we apply multiple frameworks simultaneously? What systemic improvements could we implement now?

THE EVOLUTION OF STRATEGIC THINKING

Twenty years ago, crisis management was about controlling information. Today, it's about understanding information flows and digital dynamics (Chapter 5).

Twenty years ago, it was about managing media. Today, it's about managing narratives across infinite channels while respecting cultural differences (Chapter 8).

Twenty years ago, it was about protecting reputation. Today, it's still actually about protecting your reputation, but now we're preparing for AI-generated threats we couldn't have imagined (Chapter 10).

The tools and frameworks continue to evolve, but the strategic thinking that underpins mastery remains constant. It's about seeing systems, not just events. It's about understanding forces, not just incidents. It's about building capability, not just managing damage.

Most importantly, it's about recognizing that crisis management isn't really about crisis management at all. It's about strategic leadership in an uncertain world.

There's a caveat to all of this, though. The strategic mind knows which tools to use when, how to adapt them to unique contexts, and, most importantly, when to throw out the playbook entirely because the situation requires something completely different.

CONCLUSION

"I just want to go back to normal," the CEO said after we'd successfully navigated a situation that could have resulted in massive layoffs.

I shook my head. "Normal is what got you here. The goal isn't to get back to normal. It's to build something so strategically resilient that crises become opportunities for you to gain a competitive advantage."

That's the difference between crisis management and strategic thinking.

Throughout this book, we've built your crisis management capabilities from the ground up. You now have the frameworks to assess situations, the tools to respond effectively, and the understanding to build resilient cultures. However, remember that frameworks can be learned, tools can be acquired, and approaches can be adopted.

Strategic thinking? That's earned through practice, pattern recognition, and the discipline to ask not just "How do we manage this crisis?" but "How do we use this crisis to become stronger than our competitors?"

The question isn't whether you'll face another crisis. The question is whether you'll be strategically prepared to transform it into something your competitors wish they had thought of first.

Crisis doesn't build character. It reveals it. But strategic thinking? That builds competitive advantage.

That's the conversation I'm interested in having.

NOTES

1. https://screenrant.com/fight-club-8-rules-explained/
2. https://www.instagram.com/reel/CmKG8kKJrdb
3. https://youtu.be/Jne9t8sHpUc
4. https://www.inc.com/entrepreneurs-organization/4-steps-for-creating-an-authentic-video-apology.html
5. https://www.inc.com/entrepreneurs-organization/how-to-minimize-brand-damage-when-disgruntled-employees-stir-pot.html
6. https://www.reddit.com/r/wholesomememes/comments/jw150x/believe_and_achieve/
7. https://www.washingtonpost.com/nation/2022/09/28/florida-ceo-postcardmania-hurricane-ian/
8. https://www.reuters.com/article/us-oil-spill-bp-apology/bp-ceo-apologizes-for-thoughtless-oil-spill-comment-idUSTRE6515NQ20100602/
9. https://www.prnewswire.com/news-releases/postcardmania-responds-to-hurricane-ian-by-sending-supplies-and-volunteers-to-help-families-in-need-301638918.html
10. https://www.startribune.com/target-ceo-brian-cornell-email-tough-few-months-uncertainty-among-workers/601345887
11. https://www.reddit.com/r/Target/comments/1kfrnnd/email_from_brian/
12. https://hbr.org/2019/05/boeing-and-the-importance-of-encouraging-employees-to-speak-up
13. https://www.transportation.gov/briefing-room/dot-penalizes-southwest-airlines-140-million-2022-holiday-meltdown

14. https://www.swamedia.com/southwest-stories/december-disruption-a-message-from-southwest-s-chief-administration-communicatio-MCHAQCMSGQFZFFXNG536FJRWDZQQ
15. https://www.forbes.com/councils/forbesbusinesscouncil/2020/09/15/how-to-keep-employee-morale-high-during-a-merger/
16. https://drucker.institute/quotes/
17. https://www.justice.gov/archives/opa/pr/wells-fargo-agrees-pay-3-billion-resolve-criminal-and-civil-investigations-sales-practices
18. https://www.reuters.com/sustainability/boards-policy-regulation/wells-fargos-long-road-lifting-195-trillion-asset-cap-2025-06-03
19. https://www.theacsi.org/wp-content/uploads/2022/11/22nov_FINANCE-STUDY.pdf
20. https://www.latimes.com/business/la-fi-wells-fargo-reputation-20161012-snap-story.html
21. https://www.cnn.com/2024/02/04/asia/deepfake-cfo-scam-hong-kong-intl-hnk
22. https://www.washingtonpost.com/travel/2025/08/05/delta-hertz-travel-ai-charges/
23. https://www.linkedin.com/feed/update/urn:li:activity:7338195779603365891/
24. https://techcrunch.com/2025/07/12/xai-and-grok-apologize-for-horrific-behavior/

ABOUT THE AUTHOR

Eden Gillott is a Strategic Advisor to C-Suites and boards, known for navigating reputational risk and sensitive change. As President of Gillott Communications, her work (always confidential and exclusively by referral) has guided Fortune 500 CEOs, startups, non-profits, celebrities, and even royalty through high-stakes moments.

A former professor, TEDx speaker, and author of four books, Eden has been featured across major broadcast, print, and digital media, including ABC, NBC, CBS, FOX News, NPR, *The New York Times*, *The Wall Street Journal*, and *The Washington Post*. Educated in business, crisis communications, and cybersecurity, she studied at Harvard and NYU.

A native Angeleno now based in Washington, D.C., she's traveled to 45+ countries, completed "Disney Bingo" (yes, every park on the planet), and is a Spartan Trifecta World Championship finisher.

www.ingramcontent.com/pod-product-compliance
Lightning Source LLC
Chambersburg PA
CBHW050503210326
41521CB00011B/2305